C000241879

# Dead Guilty

A play

# Richard Harris

Samuel French — London
New York - Toronto - Hollywood

## DEAD GUILTY

First performed with the title **MURDER ONCE DONE**
by Elysian Productions at the Haymarket Theatre,
Basingstoke, on 17th March 1994 with the following cast:

| | |
|---|---|
| **Julia Darrow** | Catherine Shipton |
| **Anne Bennett** | Hilary Crane |
| **Gary** | Garry Roost |
| **Margaret Haddrell** | Elizabeth Power |
| **Voice of the Coroner** | Gerald Sim |

Directed by Adrian Reynolds
Designed by Elroy Ashmore
Lighting design by David Ripley

Subsequently presented by Bill Kenwright at the Theatre
Royal, Windsor and the Thorndike Theatre, Leatherhead,
then at the Apollo Theatre, London from 17th July 1995,
with the following cast:

| | |
|---|---|
| **Voice of the Coroner** | Barry Cookson |
| **Anne Bennett** | Angela Morant |
| **Julia Darrow** | Jenny Seagrove |
| **Gary** | Niall Refoy |
| **Margaret Haddrell** | Hayley Mills |

Directed by Auriol Smith
Designed by Alexander McPherson
Lighting design by Joe Atkins

# CHARACTERS

**Julia Darrow**
**Margaret Haddrell**
**Gary**
**Anne Bennett**
**The Coroner** (voice only)


The action takes place in Julia Darrow's small Victorian house in West London


Time — the present

Other plays by Richard Harris published
by Samuel French Ltd:

Albert
The Business of Murder
Is It Something I Said?
Keeping Mum
Local Affairs
The Maintenance Man
Outside Edge
Partners
Party Piece
Stepping Out
Visiting Hour

# ACT I

*The sitting-room of Julia Darrow's small late-Victorian house in West London*

*The room is not expensively furnished but attractive, tasteful if a little untidy. There are two archways. One,* R, *is partly filled by a wooden shelf and cupboard unit, upstage of which is the open entrance to the kitchen, most of which is unseen but in which cupboards, wall units, and a window with venetian blind are visible. The second archway, upstage, leads into a small hallway which in turn leads to an unseen bedroom,* R, *and staircase,* L. *Upstage of the bedroom door, a smaller archway gives on to the main door which, like its surrounds, has stained glass windows. To the side of the door, an antique umbrella stand.* L, *a "broken" wall leads, via what would be french windows, into a glazed conservatory which gives on to the partly-visible garden. Above the conservatory, upstage, is the sash window to a bedroom which has curtains permanently, but not quite fully, drawn*

*Downstage in the sitting room is a small Chesterfield sofa with assorted scatter cushions and a folded car blanket over its back, a small buttonback chair and a coffee table with a small pile of magazines at one end. The shelf unit is packed with books, ornaments, a CD player and discs and piles of magazines.* L *of the upstage archway is a small occasional table with ornaments and plants.* L *of this table is the unseen door into a bathroom. In front of the stairs is a small antique chest of drawers holding a table lamp, telephone and answering machine. There are pictures and prints on most walls. The upstage archway has a wall light at each side*

*Upstage in the conservatory are a drawing board, draughtsman's chair, a board with notices pinned on it, plan rolls, a medium-sized, somewhat battered portfolio — all the paraphernalia of a graphic designer. There is a somewhat haphazard collection of potted plants. Downstage, two tables have been arranged L-shaped and contain more tools of the trade: a laptop computer, paper, card, a Swan Morton cutting knife, many pencils and pens, a large pair of paper scissors, an anglepoise lamp and a cordless telephone; there are also an opened envelope, a bottle of pills, a Cambridge blue vase holding flowers and an opened bottle of red wine and a glass. Under the table is a waste paper basket*

*When the* CURTAIN *rises the stage is entirely dark. Then we become aware of the distant sound of an approaching car. The engine noise gets louder and*

*louder, there is the sound of tyres screaming, then a crash; the car horn
sounds and then there is sudden silence*

*A spot comes up on Julia Darrow, isolating her in a pool of light. She sits in
a wheelchair, looking straight ahead, withdrawn*

**Coroner's Voice** You are Julia Darrow and you live at number 32, Lexham
Gardens, SW6.
**Julia** Yes.
**Coroner's Voice** As I understand it, you were a business associate of the
deceased.
**Julia** Yes. I'm a freelance graphic designer and John — Mr Haddrell — was
the art director of one of the agencies for whom I work.
**Coroner's Voice** Thank you. Now if you could tell us, in your own words,
what happened that night, and, Miss Darrow, I know this must be very
distressing for you but please remember that no-one in this court is on trial:
we are here purely and simply to ascertain the cause of death.

*A moment*

**Julia** We'd been to see a client — in Manchester. John — Mr Haddrell —
was driving and everything seemed perfectly normal — we were, you
know, we were just talking — about the meeting we'd had — just —
making conversation and then — and then he made a sort of — gasping
noise and — fell forward across the wheel and the car went out of control
and ... the next thing I knew, I was in hospital and, er, sometime later,
someone told me that John had had a heart attack. I'm sorry, that's — that's
all I can tell you.

*A moment*

*The Lights come up on the room. It is sunny. Anne Bennett is with Julia,
standing, Her summer raincoat is lying across the arm of the sofa*

**Anne** (*brightly*) So. How are you?
**Julia** (*lightly*) I thought that was for you to tell *me*.
**Anne** (*smiling*) Oh, I see ... it's going to be one of those sessions, is it?
**Julia** I'll try to be a good girl — promise.
**Anne** (*sitting on the sofa*) Are you sleeping any better?
**Julia** If I take enough pills. Not really, no.
**Anne** And you're still having the same nightmare.
**Julia** Yes, it's the same one: *I'm* driving the car, *I* cause the crash, *I* killed
him, all right?
**Anne** But you know that isn't true.

**Julia** "So why don't you say it?" Right, I'll say it: I wasn't driving the car, I didn't cause the crash — it wasn't my fault — I shouldn't feel guilty. Right. We've done that one. Next.

*A moment*

**Anne** How's the leg — d'you still get a lot of pain?
**Julia** It depends. Sometimes. Not so much now. They say it'll stop after the operation. I've still got to have one more operation.
**Anne** Does that worry you?
**Julia** The thought of another operation? Good God no, I look forward to it, it's my big treat, I'm hooked. I've been wheeled in and out so often they're making me A Friend Of The Operating Theatre, I get a discount, two femurs re-broken for the price of one and if I'm a really good girl they throw in another couple of nuts and bolts for my pelvis. What is it they say? A healthy mind in a healthy body — well, you've got the mind and they've got the body. How do *you* think it's shaping up?

*Gary enters through the main door, carrying his key and a small package. He moves confidently into the room, stuffing the key into the pocket of his hooded bomber jacket. He reacts on seeing the two women*

**Gary** (*to Julia, of Anne*) Oh I'm sorry — I thought you said twelve o'clock the lady was coming.
**Anne** (*lightly*) She was — she got her appointments back to front. Hallo — I'm Anne, Anne Bennett. You must be Gary.
**Julia** You see, Gary? You're famous.

*For a moment, it seems that Gary doesn't quite know how to take this*

**Gary** I'm really sorry, I didn't mean to butt in like ——
**Julia** It's all right, Gary. What did you want?
**Gary** It's the 28th; I collected your prescription.
**Julia** What a memory you've got, Gary, and what a little treasure you are. Isn't he a little treasure? Not only does he clean the house and do the garden, he even remembers when to collect my precious little pills — what would I do without you, Gary? (*She reaches up to touch his arm*)
**Gary** (*grinning, pleased as punch*) She calls me her daily male. Don't you, Jules?
**Julia** Yes, indeed I do. Aren't I the witty one.
**Gary** That's because I come in every day — and I'm a fellah. (*He indicates the package*) Anyway, I'll, umm — I'll put it here.
**Julia** (*suddenly sharp*) Yes, yes — just put it down and go — you know where the money is.

**Gary** (*clearly embarrassed at the sharpness, putting the package on the occasional table*) No that's all right, I'll do it next time. See you tomorrow then, Jules — and I really am very sorry for — interfering. (*He makes to go*)

**Julia** (*wanting to make amends for her sharpness towards him*) Gary, there is something you can do for me while you're here — that is, if you want to.

**Gary** (*brightening instantly*) Course I do; what is it?

**Julia** I need something to go to the cleaners; could you take it for me?

**Gary** Course I could.

**Julia** Thanks — it's in the bedroom, I won't be a minute.

**Gary** I'll get it.

**Julia** (*pulling herself out of the wheelchair*) No, that's all right, I know where it is. (*To Anne*) You don't mind?

**Anne** Of course I don't mind.

**Julia** Thanks, Gary.

*Julia smiles at him and, walking with a slight limp, exits into the bedroom*

*Gary, awkward at being left alone with Anne, moves to stand near the work table, absently taking up the knife to tap it on the table as he looks out of the window at the garden*

**Anne** (*aware of Gary's awkwardness and attempting to relieve it*) You're very fond of her, aren't you?

**Gary** (*awkwardly*) Yeah, well, she's — yeah I am, yeah.

**Anne** I know she thinks a lot of you.

**Gary** (*pleased*) Has she said?

**Anne** Not in so many words, but ——

**Gary** (*suddenly changing tone*) You shouldn't come here, why do you come here, you only upset her.

**Anne** (*thrown momentarily; then, evenly*) I'm afraid that "upsetting" her is part of the ——

**Gary** She doesn't want you here, none of you.

**Anne** (*trying to lighten it*) How d'you mean, none of me?

**Gary** These so-called friends of hers, that's why she stopped 'em coming here, they upset her, she doesn't trust 'em.

**Anne** I don't understand: doesn't trust them what?

**Gary** She doesn't *trust* 'em ... if you really want to know, she doesn't trust anyone. Except me. She trusts me, she doesn't need anyone else.

*A moment*

**Anne** Gary — you do know that when she was in hospital she tried to kill herself?

**Gary** (*frowning and giving a little shrug as though the thought is too painful to contemplate*) Yeah, well ... that's why you should leave her alone.

**Anne** No, Gary ... that's why I come here.

*Julia enters carrying some of her clothing*

**Julia** Sorry, I couldn't find my blue sweater, I could have sworn I put it with the others — you haven't moved it, have you, Gary?

**Gary** No, course I haven't.

**Julia** Oh well ... (*She gives him the clothing* ) Hang on, I'll give you some money.

**Gary** No no, give it to me later with the other.

**Julia** I hope you're keeping a tab of how much I owe you.

**Gary** (*grinning*) Don't you worry, I won't let you get away with anything.

**Julia** Anyway ... thanks — you're a love. (*And, whether for her benefit or his, we don't know, she gives Gary a quick peck on the cheek*)

*Gary reacts, pleased as punch, glancing at Anne*

Go on — off you go.

**Gary** See you tomorrow afternoon then, Jules.

**Julia** (*nodding, then realizing; what follows is clearly an off-the-cuff excuse*) No, not the afternoon, I, umm, there's someone bringing me some work over and I don't want to be disturbed.

**Gary** (*slightly surprised*) We said I'd do the garden tomorrow afternoon — it's in my diary. (*He pulls out his little pocket diary and refers to it during the following*)

**Julia** Yes I know — sorry — we'll have to change it.

**Gary** That's all right, I'll come in the morning, 'bout dinner-time, 'bout twelve o'clock — OK?

**Julia** As long as you're away by half-two.

**Gary** I could come later if you like — say about ——

**Julia** For God's sake, Gary, twelve o'clock will be fine, now go home — please.

*This moment*

*Gary looks at Anne as if to say "You see what I mean?" and then exits*

**Julia** Why does he always turn a simple yes or no into a twenty-minute conversation?

**Anne** He's only trying to be helpful. Don't you think?

**Julia** What I think is that sometimes he's too bloody helpful, sometimes he
... (*But her irritation suddenly subsides*) Look — I'm sorry. I hate the way
I am, I hate what's happening to me. I just — I don't know, I just ... . (*She
sits at the work table, looks out of the window*)

*A moment*

**Anne** (*moving nearer to Julia*) There's nothing you want to talk to me about.
**Julia** (*absently*) Like what?
**Anne** I sense — I sense that you're very uneasy today. Much more so
than ——
**Julia** ... You sense, you sense — why can't you speak like a human being
instead of all this half-baked mumbo-jumbo? Look, I'm sorry but I really
don't feel up to it today, I really don't feel like talking, I really think you
should go — in fact, I really don't see the point of you coming here any
more. (*She gets up and moves to stand with her back to Anne, looking out
over the garden*)
**Anne** When was the last time someone came to see you? Not me, not the
doctor, not Gary — a friend. When was the last time you had a friend here?
**Julia** (*looking off*) I've no idea.
**Anne** When?
**Julia** I don't need anybody. I never have. I like — sorting things out for
myself.
**Anne** But you do know there's a difference between sorting yourself out and
cutting yourself off.
**Julia** I'll see my friends when I feel more — receptive. Fair enough?
**Anne** (*smiling*) Fair enough. (*She holds her smile*)
**Julia** (*smiling too; then*) Please. I really would like you to go.
**Anne** Then I'll go. (*She takes up her summer coat*) Do I see you next week
— yes or no?
**Julia** (*managing a smile*) If you're prepared to risk it, I am.
**Anne** (*smiling*) I had one client throw a chair at me.
**Julia** You should have thrown it back.
**Anne** How do you know I didn't?

*They both smile*

**Julia** Anne ... you're right. There is something. She's written to me. His
wife, John's wife. She wants to see me. She wants to talk to me.
**Anne** Ah.
**Julia** What good will it do? I mean, for God's sake, I've never met the
woman. I — I scarcely knew *him* — what does she want me to say? What
can I tell her? He had a heart attack and died, what else does she want to
know?

*A moment*

**Anne** You see, when we lose someone close to us and we're not with them, we often need to find a way to be part of that death. To — share it.

**Julia** You're saying I should see her.

**Anne** I'm saying I can understand why she wants to see *you*. But I can also understand why you don't want to see *her*. Look, why don't we sit down and ——

**Julia** No. I'd like you to go. Really.

*This moment*

**Anne** (*taking up her bag*) I'll phone you. And in the meantime ... I suggest that you don't do anything until you and I have talked it through. Agreed?

*A moment*

*Julia nods. Anne gives her a smile and moves towards the front door; Julia remains standing by the work table*

**Julia** But you see the thing is .... (*Whatever she was going to say, she decides against. She shakes her head*) It doesn't matter.

*This moment*

*Anne doesn't pursue it. She exits, closing the front door*

*Julia stands still for a moment, then takes an opened envelope from under a pile of papers on the table. As she stands looking at it:*

*Black-out*

*Julia goes into the kitchen*

*Margaret Haddrell enters*

*A small gift-wrapped plant is placed on the coffee table and the wheelchair is set back next to the occasional table. Margaret's bag is set on the sofa*

*The Lights come up. It is a sunshine-bright day. Margaret Haddrell stands near the sofa, looking out over the garden*

*From the kitchen, there comes the sound of crockery being set on a tray. Margaret moves to sit on the sofa*

*After a moment, Julia comes through from the kitchen, carrying a tray of tea things*

*Immediately, Margaret is on her feet*

**Margaret** Can you manage?
**Julia** Yes, I'm fine.

*Margaret sits. Julia carries the tray to the work table and pours tea during the following*

**Margaret** I'm sorry, that was rude of me. I didn't mean to ——
**Julia** It's all right. Really. (*She even manages a smile. She is very tense in the presence of this woman*)
**Margaret** It's a beautiful little garden. Do you look after it yourself?
**Julia** I did. Before the — before the accident. Now someone does it for me, I just sort of — potter. (*She holds out a cup and sugar bowl*)
**Margaret** Thank you.
**Julia** Sugar?
**Margaret** No thank you.

*It's all so stiff, overly-formal. Julia sits at the work table during the following*

**Margaret** I find it very therapeutic.
**Julia** Sorry?
**Margaret** Looking after the garden.
**Julia** Oh. Yes. Do you have a — large garden?
**Margaret** Large enough. It was one of the reasons we bought the house. Not that John was much of a gardener. Mow the lawn and that was about it. (*She smiles*)

*Julia attempts one in return*

And this is where you work, is it?
**Julia** Yes. Well no, not usually; my office — workroom — is through there. (*She indicates*) For the moment I'm not very good on the stairs, so Gary moved my bed down into the office and we brought my bits and pieces out here. Luckily there's a downstairs loo and a shower so … it could have been a lot worse.
**Margaret** (*smiling, but then looking more serious*) But you will get better, will you, you will be able to ——
**Julia** Good God I hope so, although there are times when I really wonder, I don't seem ——

**Margaret** But in a way — and please don't misunderstand me when I say this — I suppose you could say you're lucky. I mean you could be like John, you could be dead — although that would have been doubly unfair, wouldn't it? I mean it was hardly your fault but then again I suppose you could say it wasn't his, it wasn't as if he was drunk or driving stupidly or something, he was taken ill, no-one could have known that was going to happen to him, he always seemed so ... he always seemed so full of life.

*This moment*

I'm so sorry.
**Julia** It doesn't matter, really, I — I understand.

*For a moment, they both seem awkward, lost for what to say, but then Margaret changes the subject*

**Margaret** (*brightly*) Gary's your "chap", is he?
**Julia** Sorry?
**Margaret** You said Gary helped you to ——
**Julia** Oh — Gary — no — Gary's my ... well, home-help, I suppose you'd call him. My — daily male.
**Margaret** Oh yes?

*Julia's half-hearted rendition of her "joke" seems to have been lost on Margaret*

**Julia** He's the one who does the garden for me. He was here just before you came, actually. That's why it's looking so — tidy.

*Margaret nods, smiles. There is an awkward moment*

**Margaret** Are the flowers from your garden?
**Julia** Yes. Past their best, I'm afraid. (*She gently touches one of the flowers in the blue vase during the following*)
**Margaret** Oh no, they're beautiful. And you don't mind cut flowers.
**Julia** No — no, not at all.
**Margaret** A lot of people do, don't they? That's why I brought you a plant, I wasn't sure.
**Julia** Thank you, it's — lovely.
**Margaret** There's a little label that tells you how to look after it.
**Julia** Yes. Thank you. (*She smiles*)

*Another awkward silence*

More tea?
**Margaret** No. Thank you.

*They smile at each other. A moment*

Quite — unusual, I would have thought. Having a ... having a man to do one's cleaning.
**Julia** Yes, I suppose it is really.
**Margaret** Is he ... you know .... (*She makes a vague gesture*)
**Julia** Gay? Not as far as I know. No, I don't think so. He knocked on the door one day, looking for work — he'd just been made redundant and he seemed genuine enough so I gave him some bits and pieces to do and, well, one job sort of led to another. Quite frankly, he's been ... well, he's been a godsend.
**Margaret** How often does he come in?
**Julia** I *pay* him for three times a week, but he comes in every day, just to see how I am and do the odd bit of shopping for me. He only lives a couple of streets away so it's not ... it's not too difficult for him. (*And she attempts to say what she's been wanting to say since the woman arrived*) Mrs Haddrell ——
**Margaret** I almost came to see you in hospital but I wasn't sure you'd ... I did look in once or twice — just to ... just to see how you were and on one occasion I very nearly made myself known to you, but ... I didn't want to upset you, I didn't want you to think I was ... Anyway. It was very good of you to answer my letter. I know it must be difficult for you and I ——
**Julia** Mrs Haddrell, I — I really don't know what I can say to you, I really don't know what you — I really don't know how anything I can tell you will — will help.

*This moment*

**Margaret** (*standing, preparing to leave*) I'm sorry. I shouldn't have written to you, I shouldn't have come here. It was selfish of me, I should have realized.
**Julia** I just don't know what I can say to you.
**Margaret** (*simply*) And I don't know ... I don't really know ... what I want you to say. I just thought — quite selfishly — I just thought that if I could speak to you, you might say something, just something, that would somehow make it ... understandable. We were together for nearly twenty years. We had our ups and downs, of course we did but — you can't live with someone that long without feeling — without feeling so very close. Without feeling — almost part of them. D'you know what my first thought was when the police came and told me he was dead? I thought, I'm sorry, you're wrong, he can't be dead, I would have known. I really did think that — oh, just for a second or two, but — I really did think that.

*This moment*

(*Smiling*) It's strange really, isn't it? Here we are, the first time we've met and it's ... so hard to talk and yet there's ... so much to say. Does that make sense or am I just being ——
**Julia** Yes. It makes sense.

*The telephone rings*

Excuse me. (*Relieved at breaking the mood, she moves to take up the telephone on the work table*)
**Julia** (*into the phone*) Hallo? ... Oh hallo Peter, can I call you back? (*She listens, then grimaces to Margaret*) Well if it won't take too long, I'm — I'm busy ... (*She cups the receiver and mouths to Margaret*) Sorry — work.
**Margaret** (*mouthing back*) Please — not at all.
**Julia** (*into the phone*) OK, go ahead. (*She makes notes with a thick pencil during the following* )

*Margaret sits. Then, unable to remain unoccupied for long, she removes the giftwrap from the plant, carefully unpeels any Sellotape, and neatly folds the paper, once, twice, three times, making rather a lot of noise in doing so, so that Julia can't really hear what is being said*

**Julia** I'll call you back. Right. Bye, Peter. (*She switches off the telephone and watches Margaret, amused despite herself*)

*Margaret finishes her immaculate folding and then looks up to see Julia watching her*

Sorry about that — work.
**Margaret** Not at all. (*Of the plant*) I unwrapped it for you.
**Julia** (*lightly*) Yes. I heard. Thank you.
**Margaret** (*holding out the folded paper*) I don't know if you save the paper.
**Julia** Umm ... no — no I don't actually. (*She takes the paper and deposits it straight into the bin under the work table*)
**Margaret** I'm dreadful like that — always have been ... wrapping paper, bits of string, even corks — goodness only knows why I should want to save corks — John says I'm —— (*She breaks off*)
**Julia** (*trying to ease the moment*) My father used to save elastic bands.
**Margaret** (*the same humourless response as to the "daily male" joke*) Oh yes?

*Julia finds herself smiling awkwardly, not quite knowing what to say*

D'you see much of them? Your parents?

**Julia** They're both dead, I'm afraid.
**Margaret** Oh. I'm sorry.

*During the following, Julia takes the tray into the kitchen, reappearing immediately*

**Julia** My mother suddenly took ill and died and my father just sort of — stopped living. He was a ... funny old chap, my dad. I'm an only child but I was never really close to him. To either of them really. (*Making an effort to brighten the conversation*) Anyway — long time ago now — and it looks like I've got a nice job, which is good.

*This moment. Neither of them seems to know what to say*

**Margaret** Well then. I must go.
**Julia** No — really, I ——
**Margaret** You have your work to do — and besides — you've had quite enough of me for one afternoon, I'm sure.
**Julia** But we've — we've hardly talked.
**Margaret** How can I explain? Knowing you were with him when he died, it was — a sort of obsession, I suppose you'd call it — wanting to meet you, wanting to ... as I said, I didn't really know what I wanted to say to you but — and please believe this — it really has helped me a lot, just — just meeting you. Thank you. I know it wasn't easy for you. (*She holds out a hand*)

*Julia takes the hand, rather formally. Then, suddenly, Margaret embraces Julia, holding her tight as though for comfort and then, as though ashamed of herself, breaks away*

I'm sorry, I'm so sorry ... goodbye ... (*She gathers up her bag and moves towards the front door*)
**Julia** (*on impulse*) Mrs Haddrell ... why don't we — why don't I telephone you and we can sit down somewhere — not here, necessarily, anywhere you like — and — talk properly?
**Margaret** Do you mean that? Do you really mean that?
**Julia** If it's — if it would help — then of course I mean it.
**Margaret** As long as you're — as long as you're quite sure. Because if you're not, I'd understand really I would and no ill feelings.

*This moment*

**Julia** Yes. I'm quite sure. I'd like to see you again.

**Margaret**  And you'll telephone me.
**Julia**  I'll telephone you.
**Margaret**  Goodbye, Miss Darrow ... and thank you.

*Margaret holds her look for a moment and then exits*

*Julia is already regretting what she has said. She stands still for a moment and then, to break her mood, moves to the CD player and presses the play button. It begins to play: something cheery from* The Marriage of Figaro

*She looks at the plant, makes up her mind, takes up the plant and exits with it into the kitchen*

*The sound of Mozart swells*

*Black-out*

*The Mozart segues into rock music*

*The blue vase of flowers is removed. The plant is moved on to the occasional table*

*The Lights come up and the music fades. Morning sunshine*

*Gary is using a "Henry"-type vacuum cleaner to clean along the back of the sofa while at the same time miming the lyric of the song coming through his personal stereo headphones*

*Julia enters from the bedroom, carrying a mug of coffee. She watches Gary, amused, sipping the coffee*

*Gary silently but enthusiastically strums the vacuum pipe guitar-wise — then becomes aware of Julia, quickly pulls off the headphones, embarrassed at being caught. Julia smiles, relaxing Gary into a grin. He switches off the cleaner and the stereo, pulls a duster from his pocket, flicks around and indicates the plant*

**Gary**  This is doing well.
**Julia**  Yes. Isn't it? That's because I'm being a very good girl and following the instructions.
**Gary**  I've been meaning to ask you where you bought it — my mum'd love something like this.
**Julia**  It was a present.

**Gary** (*grinning, clearly not believing her*) Oh yeah, who from?
**Julia** My boyfriend.
**Gary** (*his grin becoming an uneasy one; trying to sound light*) I thought you
said you didn't have no boyfriend.
**Julia** I was lying. I'm a terrible liar, Gary. You must never believe a word
I say. Just you remember that.
**Gary** (*holding the uneasy grin, unsure; then changing the subject*) D'you
want me to do upstairs?
**Julia** Not much point, is there?
**Gary** Could probably do with it, I haven't been up there for a fortnight.

*During the following, Julia takes up the mug and moves to look for something
on the work table. In doing so, she accidentally knocks the cutting knife to the
floor*

**Julia** No — don't bother — do it next time — Mrs Bennett will be here in
a minute.

*Gary automatically makes to pick the knife up for Julia*

Careful ... it's very sharp.
**Gary** (*carefully retrieving the knife and holding it up*) Like one of them
whaddyacallits, doctor's knives — scalpels — innit?
**Julia** They're pretty much the same, yes, except this is for cutting up
cardboard, not bodies, so don't get any funny ideas.
**Gary** (*still looking at the knife*) *I* wouldn't have minded being a doctor.
(*Quite suddenly, he mimes a little slashing motion, but just as soon is
grinning and putting the knife carefully on the table*) Fat chance of that
though, eh?

*During the following, Julia reads a typed letter and Gary flicks around with
the duster*

**Julia** You should have been a woman.
**Gary** Should have what?
**Julia** The number of times you change your mind. I thought it was only us
girls who did that.
**Gary** I don't understand. Sorry.
**Julia** (*looking up from her reading*) Last week you wanted to be in
computers. The week before, it was horticulture. This week it's medicine.

*He looks blankly at her*

It's a joke, Gary, a little joke.

**Gary** (*holding his blank look for a moment then attempting a smile*) Oh, yeah
  — right. (*He starts gathering up the vacuum cleaner*) I'd better get on and
  out of your way before that Mrs Bennett comes.
**Julia** Please.

*Gary takes the vacuum cleaner into the kitchen*

*The doorbell sounds*

*Gary re-enters*

**Gary** That'll be her now, will it? I'll let her in. (*He makes for the door*)
**Julia** Gary — if it's anyone else, I'm not in, OK?

*He looks at her, not understanding, and opens the front door*

*Anne is outside*

**Anne** Good-morning.

*Julia is clearly relieved to hear Anne's voice*

**Gary** (*flat*) Morning. (*He stands to one side*)

*Anne moves into the room*

*Gary exits into the kitchen during the following*

**Anne** I'm sorry — I'm a little early.
**Julia** (*expansively*) No problem.
**Anne** How have you been?
**Julia** Fine — wonderful — great — how have *you* been?

*Gary emerges from the kitchen with his bomber jacket*

**Gary** Right. I'll be away then — there's nothing you want me to bring in?
**Julia** No, I'm fine.
**Gary** See you tomorrow then. (*He nods to Anne and makes to exit*)
**Julia** (*not heavily*) Oh and Gary — thanks for telling me about the vase.
**Gary** What vase?
**Julia** The vase you broke.
**Gary** What vase?
**Julia** The little blue vase the flowers were in — you know perfectly ——

**Gary** (*seemingly mortified at the accusation*) I haven't touched it.
**Julia** Oh come on, Gary, it was in the bin. Look, I don't mind, honestly, I'm
    just surprised you didn't say anything.
**Gary** Because I didn't do it.
**Julia** Well who did? Icky The Fire Bobby?
**Gary** If I'd broken something, I would have said.
**Julia** All right, all right, it doesn't matter, it wasn't worth anything anyway,
    it was just a ——
**Gary** It wasn't me, I'm telling you, it wasn't me!

*This moment*

**Julia** Look, I'm sorry I mentioned it; goodbye, Gary.
**Gary** Yeah, but you can't ...
**Julia** Goodbye, Gary.

*This moment*

> *Gary shoots a look at Anne and moves out of the women's sight to the front
> door. He stands for a moment and then exits*

I don't understand him. Why doesn't he just say, for God's sake?
**Anne** I don't know. He seemed ——
**Julia** He seemed what? You think I made it up? You think I'm lying? Or
    what? Just what *do* you think? (*She holds her look at Anne, but then holds
    up her hands in an exaggerated gesture of surrender*) I'm sorry — all
    right? I'm sorry. (*And she "smiles" and sits "dutifully"* ) So.
**Anne** (*sitting*) Last time I was here — you told me that his wife had written
    to you. We were going to talk about whether you should ——
**Julia** Yes — well — too late, I'm afraid. I've seen her.
**Anne** Ah.
**Julia** Ah what?
**Anne** You surprise me.
**Julia** Oh yes? (*She moves to the bookshelves so that her back is to Anne*)
**Anne** Yes — last time time we spoke ——
**Julia** I wanted to get it over with. That seems reasonable enough. (*She moves
    an ornament from one shelf to another*)

*A moment*

**Anne** And how was it?
**Julia** It was like you said. She just — needed to see me. She said it was like
    an obsession. Anyway. It seems to have satisfied her. Just meeting me.

**Anne** And you?
**Julia** I hated it.
**Anne** Not her?
**Julia** Why should I hate her?
**Anne** For making you relive an event you'd rather not relive.
**Julia** I didn't have to say yes, did I? I didn't have to say yes — and now it's your turn to say "So why did you?"; I don't know, all right? I don't know.

*This moment*

The thing is — it wasn't just the once. I've seen her again.
**Anne** Whose idea was that?

*A moment*

**Julia** Mine.
**Anne** You suggested it.
**Julia** *Yes.*
**Anne** D'you know why?
**Julia** I felt — sorry for her. She looked — so lost. So lonely.

*This moment*

**Anne** D'you want to tell me about her?
**Julia** We just sort of — talk. About him. About John. But mostly — mostly she wants to know — what I can remember about that day. That last day.

*This moment*

**Anne** I don't understand. If it was so difficult for you to see her the first time, why would you submit yourself to ——
**Julia** You're right, I must have been mad — all right? I must have been bloody mad! (*Softer now*) What could I do, for God's sake, what could I say? I just feel so — so responsible.
**Anne** Why responsible?

*This moment*

**Julia** (*finally admitting*) I lied to you when I said I scarcely knew him. John. We were having an affair. That's why I was with him in the car, we were — we were going to spend the night together.

*If she was expecting a reaction, she doesn't get one*

You're not surprised.

**Anne**  No. I'm not surprised. And she didn't know.

**Julia**  Of course she didn't know. No-one knew. It's almost like a dirty joke, isn't it — the middle-aged man and his bit of stuff on the side, off for a dirty weekend — and what happens? He has a heart attack. I mean, you've got to laugh, haven't you, lady? But the thing is, isn't it, the thing is, if we hadn't been together, if we hadn't been in that particular place at that particular time, there might just have been a chance — he might just still be alive — mightn't he? Mightn't he? He might just still be alive.

**Anne**  (*firmly*) No. You heard what the pathologist said: he could have died anywhere, at any time. So why don't we can the guilt on that one and put it where it belongs. Yes?

*This moment*

**Julia**  (*sitting in the small chair*) I really know how to make things easy for myself, don't I? (*She manages a rueful little smile*)

**Anne**  Are you seeing her again?

**Julia**  Yes.

**Anne**  You're not thinking of telling her.

**Julia**  About John and me? God no. The grieving widow? That's all she'd want to hear. Apart from anything else — she seems to think they were Mr and Mrs Perfect.

**Anne**  What about you?

*Julia looks at her*

How did *you* feel about him? Did you love him?

*A moment*

**Julia**  No. We — served a purpose for each other. Perhaps if I had loved him ... but like this it's, it's somehow worse, I somehow feel — unclean.

*This moment*

**Anne**  You do realize the — problems of striking up a relationship with this woman.

**Julia**  I — don't see that I can stop it now.

**Anne**  It might be better if you did.

**Julia**  I feel I owe it to her.

**Anne**  What if she were to find out about you and her husband?

**Julia**  You don't really think I'd tell her, do you?

**Anne**  What if she found out anyway?

**Julia** How? How could she find out? No-one knew, we were — we were very careful.

**Anne** But it could happen. These things do. How do you think she'd feel *then*?

*This moment*

**Julia** (*quietly*) I've told you: she's lost and she's lonely … and I'm responsible.

*This moment*

**Anne** Well just remember … the longer it goes on, the harder it will be to extricate yourself. And the more tempted you'll be to tell her.

*This moment*

*Black-out*

*Anne exits; Margaret comes on*

*The Lights come up*

*Margaret is with Julia. Margaret is holding out a small bunch of shop flowers*

**Julia** (*taking them*) Really, you shouldn't.
**Margaret** They were so lovely I couldn't resist.
**Julia** Yes. Yes they are. Thank you. I'll just … (*She indicates the kitchen*)

*Julia exits with the flowers*

*Margaret looks around the room, automatically straightening a couple of cushions, and sits neatly on the sofa*

**Margaret** (*calling*) You did say freesias were your favourite.
**Julia** (*off*) Did I?
**Margaret** Last time I was here. You were saying how you'd love to grow them but how impossible they were without a greenhouse.

*Julia appears and stands in the archway*

**Julia** I said that?
**Margaret** (*turning to look at her; lightly*) Don't you remember? We were standing there, by the window ——

**Julia** (*with an edge*) No, I don't remember. I seem to forget a great many things nowadays. Anyway. Thank you, they're lovely. (*A moment*) Would you like a cup of tea or something?

**Margaret** Not just now: come and sit down. (*She smiles and pats the seat next to her*)

*Mildly irritated by the gesture, Julia sits, but in the chair*

How's the work going?

**Julia** I've been pretty busy, thank God.

**Margaret** That's good, although, if you don't mind my saying so, you're looking a little tired: you're not over-doing it, are you?

**Julia** When you're freelance you have to grab whatever's going.

**Margaret** You don't strike me as a grabber.

**Julia** (*lightly*) Oh, I'll grab anything I can. (*She becomes aware of the implication of what she has just said*)

*A moment*

**Margaret** I've been putting out some feelers, actually. About work, going back to work.

**Julia** Oh?

**Margaret** Yes. It seems that John didn't leave me — quite as well off as was at first imagined. He seems to have umm ... well, I don't want to sound disloyal but he, umm, he seems to have dipped into several of the insurance policies.

**Julia** Oh. I'm sorry.

**Margaret** Obviously there were — financial pressures I didn't know about. He didn't — involve me in that side of things. Ours was that sort of marriage, I'm afraid: not terribly — modern. John was the breadwinner — and I was the cakebaker. (*She smiles brightly but then, almost instantly*) It's my fault: he should never have gone on that trip, he didn't want to — he said to me: "I just don't feel like going". Something was worrying him, he wouldn't say what, but he was so — edgy and I told him not to be silly, that it was business, that he must go. He did die instantly, didn't he? He wouldn't have felt anything, would he? Would he? (*She looks pleadingly at Julia*)

*Julia can offer nothing. This moment*

(*Becoming calmer*) But that's what it so often comes down to, isn't it? If only I'd said this. If only I'd done that. If only I could rewrite the story and give it a happy ending.

**Julia** Margaret ——
**Margaret** No. Don't say anything. Please. Now where were we? Oh yes. I said I might have to go back to work.

*A moment*

**Julia** (*attempting normality*) What will you do?
**Margaret** The only thing I know anything about, I suppose. Nursing. I was a nurse. That's how I met John, I was looking after someone he knew.

*The telephone rings*

**Julia** (*relieved*) That'll be the agency — sorry. (*She goes to the work table and picks up the telephone*) Yes? ... Oh, hallo Peter. ... Fine. ... Must it be right now, I'm with someone. ... Oh, I see, well, just a minute, let me get a pad ... (*She cups the receiver; mouthing to Margaret*) Sorry.
**Margaret** (*miming back*) Please.

*Julia takes up a large notepad and thick pencil*

(*Indicating the kitchen; mouthing*) I'll put the flowers in water, shall I?

*Julia absently nods her thanks, her mind on her work*

*Margaret exits into the kitchen*

**Julia** (*into the phone*) Right — with you. (*She makes notes during the following*) Is this for a full page or half page? No, don't tell me, let me guess: really bold lettering, plenty of spacing, white on black — when does he ever want anything different? Oh yeah, what about the logo, are we using the same one? ... Right. ... A couple of roughs ... by when? ... No, no that's fine, what will you do, send a bike? ... (*She laughs freely at something he says*) ... If I'm finished earlier, I'll let you know. ... Bye Peter. ... Thanks. (*She switches off the telephone*)

*Margaret comes in from the kitchen with the flowers in the blue vase. She looks around, choosing where to put them*

(*Jotting notes, still smiling at the thought of what was said to her*) I'm sorry about that.
**Margaret** No no, not at all, you have to do your work. Mmmm ... they smell quite lovely. Is it all right if I put them here? (*The coffee table*)
**Julia** (*not really looking*) That's fine, yes, thanks.

**Margaret** (*setting the vase down on the coffee table and then adjusting its position a fraction*) I did try to find a smaller vase but this was the only one I could see.

**Julia** Sorry?

**Margaret** Sorry — I was just saying I think they would have looked better in a smaller vase but I couldn't find one.

**Julia** No, I'm sure they'll be ... (*For the first time, she turns her full attention to the flowers and reacts on seeing the vase*) Where was — did you get that?

**Margaret** I'm sorry?

**Julia** The vase — where did you get the blue vase?

**Margaret** It was — on the side. Near the blender.

**Julia** But it couldn't have been, it was broken.

**Margaret** (*looking at the vase, confused, but maintaining her politeness*) I'm so sorry — would you prefer that I ... (*She takes up the vase, as if to return it to the kitchen*)

**Julia** (*clearly in a mild state of shock*) No. No. That's — fine.

*Margaret replaces the vase, carefully choosing its position. Julia remains looking at it during the following, her mind very much on the mystery of the vase*

**Margaret** Would you be angry if I said I'd told you a little fib? When we first met. Well, not so much a fib, more ... well, I thought if I told you the truth, you might think I was — well, peculiar. (*She smiles her smile — the smile of an insecure woman who desperately needs to be liked*)

**Julia** How d'you mean — peculiar?

**Margaret** I said that I wanted to meet you because I wanted you to tell me about John, about what happened that day ... but that isn't quite true. I had it in my head that he wanted to communicate with me, that because you were the last one to see him alive, he would do it through you.

*A moment*

**Julia** And did he?

**Margaret** Let's say — I feel his presence.

*A moment. Julia looks at Margaret; Margaret turns and sees this look*

(*Smiling*) You don't believe there's a life hereafter.

**Julia** I often don't believe there's a life before. No. No I don't.

**Margaret** I do, you see. Because — when you've been that close to someone, they never really go away. As long as you remember them, they never really die.

**Julia** Margaret, this is going to sound terribly rude, but — that telephone call:
the agency wants some work done rather quickly and ——

**Margaret** (*anxiously*) And you want me to go — yes of course.

**Julia** Well no ... not — not right now, but — soon. I'm sorry.

**Margaret** Don't be silly. Tell you what: we'll have that cup of tea and then
I'll go; all right?

**Julia** (*smiling*) Fine.

**Margaret** No, no I'll do it — you stay where you are. In fact — why don't
you start your work now? Go on, I won't mind; I'd like it, truly.

*A moment. Then Julia smiles and moves dutifully to sit at her work table. She
gets involved in her work, only half-listening to the following*

(*Pleased*) There. (*She makes to go into the kitchen, but stops*) Oh yes: I
asked my neighbour why she so detested cut flowers.

**Julia** (*flat*) Oh?

**Margaret** It's all to do with beauty being cut down in its prime. Apparently
in some countries they're regarded as a sign of impending death.

*Margaret exits into the kitchen*

*Julia looks up, realizing what has been said, and turns her head towards the
kitchen*

*Black-out*

*Gary enters*

*The Lights come up*

*Gary, wearing his jacket, is with Julia; she stands at the work table, pointing
towards the vase*

**Julia** Gary — listen to me, will you? Last week, I found that vase — broken
— in the wastebin. Yesterday, it's on the side, next to the blender. Explain
that to me, will you?

**Gary** I don't know.

**Julia** Gary — explain it to me.

**Gary** I don't know.

**Julia** You didn't break that vase and replace it.

**Gary** No — and I didn't see it in the bin, neither!

**Julia** (*softly*) What are you saying?

**Gary** I'm saying: you saw it in the bin, I didn't.

*This moment*

**Julia** (*softly*) All right, Gary. Thanks.
**Gary** Yeah ... well, I'll get on with a bit of weeding while I'm here.

*He moves towards the french windows*

**Julia** Not now — sorry. I've got someone coming.
**Gary** What — that Mrs Bennett?
**Julia** No, not Mrs Bennett. A friend.
**Gary** What friend?
**Julia** (*half-laughing at his cheek*) Gary — mind your own.
**Gary** I thought you didn't want to see any of your friends — what's so special about this one?
**Julia** Gary ——
**Gary** That lady, is it?
**Julia** (*caught on the hop*) What lady? What lady, Gary?

*Now it's Gary's turn to be caught*

**Gary** That lady who comes here.
**Julia** What lady who comes here?
**Gary** I've seen her, haven't I?
**Julia** (*trying to keep things light*) Have you been spying on me?
**Gary** No I have not! I just — seen her.
**Julia** You have — you've been spying on me.
**Gary** I haven't! I was going by and she was getting out of her car. I seen her knock.
**Julia** Yes, that's right, Gary. That lady.
**Gary** You could've told me about her.
**Julia** What d'you mean, I could have ——
**Gary** Why didn't you tell me about her?
**Julia** (*quietly*) Because what I do and who I see is none of your bloody business. (*She holds her look at him*)

*The doorbell rings*

(*Quietly and very politely*) That'll be her now: let her in on your way out please, Gary.

*She takes up the vase and goes into the kitchen*

*Gary stands, awkwardly, aware that he has gone too far, then moves quickly to the door and opens it*

*Margaret is outside. She is holding a cake tin and her handbag. She enters the room*

*Gary stands back to let Margaret come in, avoiding looking at her, and then exits, closing the door*

*Margaret turns to watch Gary go and then moves into the room*

*Julia comes out of the kitchen*

**Julia** *(attempting a smile and an excuse)* Sorry, I was er … *(She vaguely indicates "in the kitchen")*
**Margaret** That was Gary, was it?
**Julia** Yes. That was Gary. *(Brightly)* How are you?
**Margaret** I've been making myself busy. *(She holds out the tin)*

*Julia instinctively takes the tin. Margaret remains where she is, clearly expecting Julia to open the tin there and then. Julia opens the tin and looks into it. A moment*

**Julia** Oh. It's a cake.
**Margaret** You do like fruit cake?
**Julia** Well, yes — it's just that … well, it's such a *big* fruit cake.
**Margaret** If you don't want it, you don't have to take it — truly. I just thought — it would be nice, and the truth is … well, the truth is, baking helps to keep things — normal. And it's nice to — have someone to do it *for.*
**Julia** It was very thoughtful of you: thank you, Margaret. *(She suddenly feels clumsy, holding the tin)* I'll just, umm …

*Julia carries the tin through into the kitchen*

*During the following, Margaret goes through her ritual of straightening a cushion or two, and repositioning an ornament on the occasional table*

**Margaret** *(calling after Julia)* If you keep it in the tin it will last for ages.
**Julia** *(off)* Right.
**Margaret** *(lightly)* Don't keep it too long though or I won't be able to bring you another one.
**Julia** *(off)* Yes — right.
**Margaret** I know what you're like, you single girls … I don't suppose you're eating half as well as you should be. *(She moves into the conservatory and looks out over the garden)*

*Julia comes in from the kitchen and sits on the sofa*

The garden's looking quite lovely. It must give you such pleasure.

**Julia** Yes. It does.

**Margaret** I've been meaning to ask you — do you grow from seed or what?

**Julia** Garden centre, I'm afraid.

**Margaret** Oh no, far too expensive. Next year you shall have some of my cuttings.

**Julia** (*after reacting slightly at the thought of "next year"*) Yes. Thank you.

**Margaret** (*still looking out at the garden*) I thought I saw him today. John. It was someone else of course. But I did, I really thought it was John. Not the John you knew, the John I first met, the John I see when I close my eyes every night, with his — black hair and his blue eyes and that lovely, lovely, smile. (*She turns and moves into the room, smiling happily as she recalls*) He really did sweep me off my feet, you know. He was so romantic. And such a charmer. A bit of an old sprucer, as my father would say. Well — you'd know how charming he could be, he never lost it, did he?

**Julia** (*awkwardly*) Yes, he ...

**Margaret** (*taking up her bag and sitting on the sofa next to Julia*) I found some old photographs — in one of his drawers. He must have kept them all these years — would you like to see them? (*She takes three or four old photographs out of her bag and passes them to Julia*)

*Julia looks unwillingly at the photographs*

(*Taking a pair of reading glasses from her bag and putting them on*) These were taken before we were married. I would have been about your age. I wasn't much of a catch even then, was I?

**Julia** Nonsense, you're very ——

**Margaret** You can see what I mean about that smile. And he was such a terrible flirt ... (*She takes one of the photographs back and regards it fondly*) ... Weren't you, you terror? Such an outrageous flirt. But then you always were. (*She returns the photograph to Julia; lightly*) I expect he flirted with *you*: you don't have to pretend — he flirted with all the pretty girls. When we were first married, I couldn't cope with it at all but then I realized that it was just his way of — well, having fun I suppose you'd say — of — making someone else feel good. That was his great strength, you know. Making other people feel good. You must have seen that.

**Julia** Yes. (*She gives the photographs back to Margaret*)

**Margaret** (*putting the photographs and her glasses back into her bag*) I do miss him so much. Perhaps if we'd had children ... the thing is though, we didn't want children. No, that isn't quite true. The subject never came up, not in the beginning and then, when we did think about it, when we did think that maybe we should ... I found I couldn't have them. (*A rueful smile*) That's ... life, as they say. (*This moment. Then, brightly changing the subject*) Are you still seeing your counsellor?

**Julia** Yes. Yes I am.

**Margaret** D'you think it helps?

**Julia** I'm — I'm not sure. I think so.

**Margaret** They offered *me* one, you know. A bereavement counsellor. I said no. I don't believe in all that, I believe one should be able to cope oneself.

**Julia** (*standing and moving away*) I'm not that strong.

**Margaret** I'm sorry, I ... I'm sorry.

*This moment*

**Julia** I suppose I feel pretty much like you do, I've always been rather sceptical of — therapists and so on, but at the time, I — I was very low and not in much of a position to argue, really. I — I'd tried to kill myself.

**Margaret** Oh my poor girl, I had no idea.

**Julia** Oh I don't think I meant to do it properly, it was just that, after the accident, everything seemed so — I dunno — so hopeless. I got hold of some pills. Luckily one of the nurses found me. Anyway ... that's ... when Anne came on the scene. (*But she realizes*) My God, listen to me — whingeing away ... how dare I?

**Margaret** If it helps you to say these things, you must say them.

**Julia** Yes, but ——

**Margaret** That's why we see each other, isn't it? I'm helping you, you're helping me.

**Julia** Margaret ... (*She is dangerously close to blurting out the truth of their relationship. But changes it*) You mustn't be so — nice to me.

**Margaret** Why ever not?

**Julia** Because — I'm not what you think I am, I'm not — worthy of too much — friendship.

*This moment*

**Margaret** (*brightly*) Oh dear me, listen to us: Moaning Minnies the pair of us, right?

**Julia** (*managing a smile*) Right.

**Margaret** Right — so what I'm going to do — is make us a cup of tea. (*She stands*) A nice cup of tea and a slice of fruit cake.

**Julia** I'll do it.

**Margaret** You most certainly will not. When *I'm* here, you put your feet up.

*Margaret starts to manœuvre Julia to sit on the sofa*

**Julia** Margaret ... I'm not an invalid. Well ... not a complete invalid.

**Margaret** (*mock-firm*) Don't — argue.

**Julia** (*smiling*) Yes, nurse.

**Margaret** That's right — "Yes nurse". Have they given you a date for the
   operation yet?
**Julia** End of the month. The 28th.
**Margaret** You will let me come and visit you, won't you?
**Julia** Of course I will.

*Despite herself, she reaches up to touch Margaret's hand*

*This moment*

**Margaret** (*moving towards the kitchen, then stopping*) Oh yes — something
   else I've been meaning to ask you: when you had the accident, you said you
   were coming back to London.

*A slight pause*

**Julia** Yes.
**Margaret** Because — silly really, but it's stuck in my mind — John phoned
   me, just before you left, it must have been, to say he wouldn't be coming
   back that night, that he was staying the night in Chester, I think he said.

*This moment*

**Julia** I meant *I* was coming back to London. John was — dropping me off
   at the station.
**Margaret** Oh. Oh I *see* ... (*She smiles brightly*) ... there's always an answer,
   isn't there?

   *She goes into the kitchen*

*This moment*

**Julia** I was fucking your husband. That's the "answer" — all right? I was
   fucking your husband.

*This moment*

*Black-out*

*A scattering of papers is set by the sofa and a chiffon scarf is draped over one
arm*

*The Lights come up. The sound of rain and a distant thunder storm. The room
is in early evening shadows. The only light is that of the anglepoise lamp*

*Julia is asleep on the sofa with her legs up and a thick marker pen still in her
hand*

*After a moment, Gary enters through the front door, using his key. He is
wearing his bomber jacket with the hood up and carrying some of Julia's
clothing in plastic from the dry cleaner's. He moves into the room,
assuming it to be empty — and sees her. He puts down the clothing and
moves to her*

**Gary** (*gently*) Jules ...

*No response. A moment. He pushes back the hood of the jacket, wipes rain
from his face and stands looking down at Julia. Then he reaches down and
takes up the chiffon scarf. He holds it in his hands, then raises it to his nose.
He remains looking down at her, then absently puts the scarf into a pocket,
carefully takes the car blanket from the back of the sofa, unfolds it and gently
puts it across Julia's legs. He bends and is gently attempting to extricate the
marker pen from her fingers when she suddenly jerks awake with a loud gasp
which in turn startles him into an equally loud gasp; he jerks away from her.
She stares at him as though not recognizing him*

**Julia** What do you want, what are you doing here? (*She gets up, moves away
from him and turns on the main lights during the following*)
**Gary** You asked me to collect the dry cleaning. (*He indicates it, then takes
up and folds the blanket*)

*Julia collects up the fallen papers, takes them to the work table, puts them
down and looks for something during the following*

**Julia** Yes — well — from now on I don't want you just — walking in and
out like you own the place — all right, Gary?
**Gary** Yeah, but you always said it was ——
**Julia** I've changed my mind, I don't *like* it — and I don't like you tiptoeing
around, wrapping me up like I'm some sort of cripple; I'm fed up with
people treating me like a cripple, all right? (*She finds what she was looking
for — a bottle of pills*) Anyway — thanks. How much do I owe you?
**Gary** Ummm ... (*He pulls a receipt from his pocket*) Seven pounds sixty.
**Julia** You know where the money is.
**Gary** That's all right, we can do it at the end of the ——
**Julia** I want to settle up *now* — all the bits and pieces I owe you — all right?
*Now.*

*Julia goes into the kitchen*

*Gary stands for a moment, then puts the receipt on the work table, moves to the small chest of drawers and opens the second drawer. He stands for a moment, then pushes the drawer closed again*

*Julia comes in from the kitchen with a glass of water*

**Julia**  Is there enough there?

**Gary**  (*awkwardly*) I can't remember how much you owe me.

**Julia**  You said you were keeping a check.

**Gary**  I am. I left it at home.

**Julia**  Oh for God's sake, Gary! (*She swallows down a couple of pills*)

**Gary**  I didn't know you'd want to settle up today, did I? We said end of the week, with my wages.

**Julia**  Tell me something: if you're so bloody hard up, how come you never seem to need any money?

**Gary**  (*quietly*) That's my business.

*This moment*

**Julia**  (*going to the work table, putting down the glass and looking at the papers*) Look — I'm sorry. I fell asleep when I should have been working and I woke up in a bad mood — there's a surprise. I'm sorry.

**Gary**  I didn't mean to frighten you.

**Julia**  I know you didn't.

**Gary**  I was just trying to ——

**Julia**  Yes, Gary — I *know*.

*This moment. Gary tries to lighten the moment, perching on the edge of the sofa and indicating the garden. During the following, he puts a hand in his pocket and realizes the scarf is there. He discreetly returns it to the arm of the sofa*

**Gary**  I was thinking: that corner bit down there — where you think needs brightening up a bit — how about if I pulled that stuff out and we put in a nice bush or something — something to give you a bit o' colour all year round?

**Julia**  Yes. Good idea.

**Gary**  D'you want me to have a look round the gardening centre?

**Julia**  No, I'll do it. Or better still, we'll go together — shall we do that?

**Gary**  (*pleased*) Yeah, great: when?

**Julia**  Umm — well — no rush is there? Some time.

*This moment*

**Gary** Right. See you tomorrow, then — oh, and I'll be in early if that's OK — say about ten o'clock. (*He makes to go*)

**Julia** Gary ... (*Not heavily*) Can you remember how many bottles of red wine there were?

**Gary** Er ... three, I think.

**Julia** That's what I thought — so what's happened to it?

**Gary** You must've drunk it.

**Julia** No, no, I had one bottle; there were two more on top of the cupboard by the fridge.

**Gary** No — you drank it.

**Julia** Gary — I had one ——

**Gary** I can show you the empty bottles.

*Julia turns away from Gary, not understanding*

There were three bottles in the bin. I took 'em out because I know you like them to go to the bottle bank.

**Julia** (*returning to sit at the work table*) Yes, all right, all right! Becoming a regular little cornucopia that wastebin, isn't it? Anything I want, anything I can't find, anything I've "mislaid", look in the bin and waddya know, there it is. Next time you're passing, see if you can find a man in there for me, will you?

*This moment*

**Gary** (*moving nearer her*) Jules ... what have I done wrong?

**Julia** What d'you mean, Gary, what have you done wrong?

**Gary** You keep accusing me of things.

**Julia** I'm not accusing you of anything.

**Gary** You do, Jules, and it really hurts me. I mean I know I'm only the bloke who comes in and cleans and everything but you can, you can be really hurtful and it's not like you, you used to be so lovely, so nice to me and there's nothing I wouldn't do for you, Jules, nothing — I'd kill for you, honest I would.

**Julia** Don't be so bloody — don't say things like that, Gary.

**Gary** I just — I just don't understand you.

*A slight moment*

**Julia** No. (*She gives him a rueful little smile*) Look — I've got some work to do. Sorry.

*This moment. Then Gary moves away and turns to stand looking at Julia. She becomes aware and turns to look at him. He quickly breaks his look*

*Gary moves to the front door, and exits*

*Julia begins working and becomes engrossed*

*The Lights change. It is an hour or so later. The room is illuminated only by the table lamps and the pool of light from the desk lamp. There is music playing softly on the CD machine*

*Julia is engrossed in her work. She automatically reaches for where her knife should be, but it isn't there. Somewhat surprised, she looks for the knife. The cordless telephone rings. She automatically takes it up, her mind very much on finding the missing knife*

(*Into the phone*) Hallo?

*There is no answer. Unconcerned, she switches off the telephone and resumes her search for the knife. The telephone rings again, and again she takes it up quickly*

(*Into the phone*) Hallo — yes?

*Again there is no answer*

Hallo? Hallo? (*Trying to sound light*) That's not you, is it Gary?

*But nothing. This time she is somewhat uneasy. She switches off the telephone and makes to pour herself a glass of wine, but the bottle is empty. She gets up and moves through the archway towards the kitchen. The telephone rings again. She snatches up the second telephone*

(*Into the phone*) Who the hell is it, what do you want? What do you want?

*Black-out*

*The music and rain sounds fade*

*The Lights come up again. It is a sunny afternoon. Julia sits at the work table, taking two large capsules from the bottle*

*Margaret comes in from the kitchen with a glass of water*

**Margaret** There.
**Julia** (*smiling her thanks and holding up one of the capsules*) Look at the size of these things. What d'they think I am — a horse?

**Margaret** May I? (*She takes the bottle and reads the printed label*)
**Julia** (*swallowing down one of the capsules*) You really shouldn't be doing all this running around, you know.
**Margaret** (*cheerily*) Nonsense. It's good practice for me. (*Of the bottle*) I hope you're careful with these: they're very strong.
**Julia** Don't worry, nurse, everything's under control. Well ... vaguely ... (*She toasts Margaret with the glass*) Cheers. (*She pops the second capsule in her mouth and swallows it down with a large grimace*)

*Margaret smiles, puts the bottle on the work table and goes through her ritual cushion-plumping during the following*

**Margaret** I've joined a nursing agency.
**Julia** That's good. Isn't it?
**Margaret** I'm going for an interview next Monday.
**Julia** Good.
**Margaret** Well. We'll see. (*She sits and smiles at Julia*)

*Julia attempts a smile in return, but there is clearly something on her mind*

Can I help?
**Julia** Sorry?
**Margaret** There's obviously something worrying you.
**Julia** No, no, I'm just ... (*Suddenly decisive*) Will you do something for me, will you look in that drawer and tell me how much money there is in there?

*Margaret looks at Julia, not understanding*

Please.

*A moment. Margaret moves to the small chest and makes to open the top drawer*

No, the next one.
**Margaret** (*opening the second drawer*) There are some notes and some change.
**Julia** How much in notes?
**Margaret** Two five pound notes. Ten pounds.

*A moment. Julia nods her thanks. Margaret puts the notes back in the drawer and closes it*

**Julia** I just wanted to make sure I wasn't — seeing things.

**Margaret** I'm sorry, I don't ——
**Julia** I think Gary's stealing money from me. There was twenty pounds in that drawer last night. After he left this morning, there was just the ten.
**Margaret** Are you sure? I mean are you quite sure, you haven't perhaps put it ——
**Julia** It isn't the first time, it's happened before. I thought perhaps I'd made a mistake.

*A moment*

**Margaret** I don't really know what to say.
**Julia** (*firmly*) I can't have him coming here any more. I'll have to get rid of him.
**Margaret** But unless you've got positive proof, you can't really accuse him of ——
**Julia** I shan't. I'll just — tell him I don't need him any more.

*This moment*

**Margaret** If you're — if you're really sure.
**Julia** It isn't just the money, it's — it's other things. My cutting knife has gone, some compact discs, pens — all sorts of things. Even — bits and pieces of my underwear. I've got a feeling he comes in here when I'm out.
**Margaret** (*sitting on the sofa*) But you've always said he's so fond of you. Why would he ——?
**Julia** I think he's jealous. Of you. I really think he's jealous of you. Well — not so much of you — of what you represent. Someone else — coming into my life. I think he wants me all to himself. It's my fault. I've let him get too close.

*This moment*

**Margaret** Perhaps — rather than — lose him — it would be better if I didn't come here any more.

*This moment. It's the time when Julia could perhaps untie the knot, but ...*

**Julia** No.
**Margaret** But you *need* him. He does so much for you.
**Julia** Then I'll just have to — re-adjust. Won't I? (*She moves into the conservatory and stands looking out over the garden*)

*This moment. Then Margaret, seemingly unable to sit still, gets up, takes up the glass, and moves towards the kitchen*

**Margaret** If you really are — telling him to go — you know that you'll always have me, don't you? You know I'll do whatever I can for you.

*This moment. Unseen by Margaret, Julia closes her eyes in quiet despair, but then gives a little nod. A moment*

*Margaret goes into the kitchen*

*Black-out*

*Gary's jacket is hung over the newel post of the stairs; an unsealed envelope containing banknotes is set on Julia's desk*

*The Lights come up. It is early afternoon. The room is empty for a moment*

*Gary appears at the head of the stairs. He moves slowly down and stops about half-way, absently running a duster along the handrail as though an uneasy thought has occurred to him. He continues down*

*The bedroom door opens and Julia enters, dressed in smart outdoor wear*

**Julia** What are you doing?
**Gary** I thought I'd do upstairs.
**Julia** Gary — I've said — no-one goes up there, there's no point, it's a waste of time. (*She moves to the work table, collects up some layouts and puts them in her portfolio*)
**Gary** (*knowing that, for some reason, he's treading on eggs; brightly*) Yeah — you're right — but I'll have to do it when you're in hospital, won't I, so when you get back it'll be all nice and clean and we can move everything upstairs again.
**Julia** Gary — I don't want you coming in here when I'm away. In fact — I'm going to have to pay you off.
**Gary** Pay me off? (*He smiles nervously*) I don't understand.
**Julia** I mean I'm going to have to do without you, Gary. I — I'm short of money. I can't afford you any more. Besides — I'm getting too dependent on you and I don't want that, I really don't want that.
**Gary** Yeah — OK — but what if I only came in once or twice a ——
**Julia** I can't afford it.
**Gary** But you know I wouldn't ——
**Julia** Don't argue with me, Gary — *please.* (*She holds out the unsealed envelope*) I'd like you to finish today. I know it's short notice so I've paid you an extra week. Take it — please.

*The doorbell sounds*

*Gary takes the envelope and looks down at it, stunned*

**Julia** That'll be my taxi. (*She looks at Gary, knowing just how stunned he is; gently*) I'm very grateful for all you've done but ... please Gary — just accept what I've said and ——

**Gary** No skin off my nose. I've got plenty of other places I'm welcome.

**Julia** Good. I'm glad.

**Gary** We'll just see how you get on without me. Or will your new friend be looking after you?

**Julia** (*stonily*) Finish what you're doing and go home, Gary — all right? Go home.

*She holds her look at Gary for a moment and then moves to the front door and exits*

*Gary remains standing still, his sudden flash of bravado evaporating. He looks down at the envelope and opens it lifelessly. He remains looking at the money, then his anger returns and he shoves the money back into the envelope, hurls the duster into the kitchen, pulls on his bomber jacket, stuffs the envelope into a pocket, takes out the house key and tosses it on to the sofa, makes to go, but has a change of mind and goes back, takes up the key and moves to the work table, takes up a pencil and paper and prepares to write something. The doorbell sounds. He freezes. Should he or shouldn't he answer it? He decides he should and moves to the door and opens it*

*Anne is outside*

**Anne** (*giving Gary a friendly smile and coming in*) Hallo. (*She moves into the room, expecting to see Julia*)

**Gary** (*not without pleasure*) You're too late.

**Anne** Sorry?

**Gary** She's not in: she's gone to one of her meetings. You just missed her.

**Anne** Oh, (*She's clearly thrown but, for his sake, decides to make light of it*) She must have forgotten I was coming.

**Gary** I doubt it.

**Anne** (*deciding not to take him up on that*) Well, if you could just tell her I came ——

**Gary** I won't have the chance, will I? She's given me the push. The elbow. The Big E.

**Anne** When did that happen?

**Gary** About ten minutes ago. I couldn't believe it.

**Anne**  Did she say why?

**Gary**  She gave me some old moody about not being able to afford it. But I think she's just looking for trouble, making things up so that she can have a go at me. I mean, you heard the way she went on about that stupid vase — not a day goes by without her accusing me of something — and now she's given me the elbow.

*A moment*

**Anne**  Well, if you do go, she'll need some sort of help, surely?

**Gary**  She's got her new friend, hasn't she?

**Anne**  What new friend?

**Gary**  That lady.

**Anne**  D'you mean Mrs Haddrell?

**Gary**  That's her — Mrs Haddrell. It's all gone wrong. Everything was really nice and then you had to interfere, didn't you, all of you. (*He holds his look at her*)

*Black-out*

   *Gary and Anne exit*

*The Lights come up. Later the same evening. The room is lit only by one of the side lights*

*There is a pause and then a shaft of light falls from the upstairs window on to the glass roof of the conservatory. A moment. The telephone rings four times; then Anne's voice comes over the answering machine*

   *During the following, we hear the key in the front door. Julia comes in carrying the portfolio*

*As Julia takes out the key and closes the door, the light goes out in the bedroom. She moves into the room, listening to the telephone message, but doesn't answer it. Instead she sits in the wheelchair next to the chest, taking off her shoes*

**Anne**  (*voice, distorted*) Julia ... it's Anne, calling at — half-nine. I'm sorry I missed you earlier — anyway, no problem — I just wanted to wish you well for the operation tomorrow: let's hope this is the last one. I'll telephone the hospital to see how you are and hope to come and see you. Bye.

*The answer machine clicks off*

*Julia remains sitting for a moment and is suddenly overwhelmed with tiredness. She takes up her shoes, rubs her painful leg, switches off the light, and goes into the bedroom*

*The room is now in shadow. This moment is held for as long as possible — then the shaft of light from the upstairs window falls on the glass roof of the conservatory again, then we see a narrow shaft of light at the top of the stairs; a door has been opened. The shaft of light widens*

*Julia, now in a light dressing-gown over nightwear, comes out of the bedroom*

*The door upstairs is closed quickly*

*Julia goes to the front door and puts on the chain, then goes back into the bedroom, closing the door*

*A moment, and then the upstairs door is opened, throwing the narrow shaft of light down the stairs ... and the shaft of light widens; in it we see the undefined outline of a figure standing in the upstairs doorway*

*This moment is held and ——*

*— the* CURTAIN *falls*

# ACT II

*The same. Late afternoon*

*When the* CURTAIN *rises the front door is open and a bag of groceries stands by the sofa. A broad beam of daylight shines through the partly-drawn curtains*

*Margaret is wheeling in Julia in her wheelchair, a pair of aluminium elbow crutches and a pile of mail — most of it junk mail — across her knees*

**Julia**  I'm all right from here, thanks.
**Margaret**  (*a little breathlessly*) Right. I'll just get your bag out of the car.

*Margaret exits again*

**Julia**  (*looking around — for all her concerns, glad to be home*) Hallo house. Have you missed me? (*She tosses the crutches on to the sofa and starts looking through the mail*)

*Margaret enters with an expensive overnight bag. She takes the key out of the door, closes the door and moves into the room*

**Margaret**  (*indicating the bag*) I'll put it straight in the bedroom, shall I?
**Julia**  Please.

*Margaret takes the bag into the bedroom*

*Julia reads one of the letters which has taken her interest*

*Margaret enters*

**Margaret**  Where shall I put the key?
**Julia**  Oh ... by the phone ... thanks.
**Margaret**  (*of the telephone answering machine*) You've got nine messages; d'you want to hear them?
**Julia**  (*still reading*) What? No — I'll do it later. Listen to this — it's from the lawyer representing the insurance company — (*she reads*) "Blah-blah-blah ... just to inform you that the matter is still in hand and that we hope

to write to you soon with some positive information". (*She gives a derisive little jerk of the head and jettisons the letter*)

**Margaret** I had more or less the same letter three days ago.

**Julia** And what does it mean? Nothing. Apart from another fifty quid on the bill. (*Brightly*) Did you know they're now using lawyers instead of rats in medical research? For three reasons, basically: one, there are more lawyers than there are rats; two, the technicians don't get as attached to the lawyers as they do to the rats; and three, there are some things a rat just won't do.

**Margaret** (*after looking at Julia rather blankly*) Oh, I see. (*She flutters a smile*) I'm not very good with jokes. I don't really understand them. Not like John. John has — had — a wonderful sense of humour. Wouldn't you say?

**Julia** (*flat*) Yes. Wonderful.

**Margaret** I think that's very attractive in a man — don't you — a good sense of humour? In fact I think in the long run it's probably the most attractive quality there is. Apart from loyalty, of course. Now then: (*she takes up the grocery bag*) bread, milk, orange juice, butter, eggs, soup — only packet, I'm afraid, I'll bring you some of my homemade tomorrow — a couple of apples and some nice cheese — you like Brie, don't you? That should keep you going, shouldn't it, and when you're ready we'll make out a list and I'll go to Waitrose and stock up for the week — it is Waitrose you use, isn't it? (*She carries the bag towards the kitchen*) I expect you'd like a cup of tea.

**Julia** No: what I'd like is a very large glass of wine but don't worry, I won't have one, I won't have anything, thank you.

*This moment*

*Margaret exits into the kitchen*

I don't *want* you here … why can't you understand? I don't *want* you here. (*She remains sitting, angry at herself for being unable to control the situation, then makes up her mind, reaches for the elbow crutches and determinedly levers herself out of the chair*)

*Margaret enters*

**Margaret** Are you sure you should be doing that? (*She watches the following with no expression in her face*)

**Julia** That's what they said: "Get yourself moving as soon as possible". So … (*she holds up the crutches*) Look Ma, I'm dancing! (*She wobbles and with a "Whoops!" regains her balance and collapses back into the chair*) Well … tomorrow maybe. (*She smiles and reaches across to put the crutches against the sofa, then looks across at Margaret*)

*Margaret turns on a fond smile*

What?

**Margaret** It's good to see you smile. I mean — really smile.

**Julia** Yes. I feel quite cheerful. Optimistic. If I'm not careful I shall turn into a half-way decent human being again. (*She smiles over-brightly at Margaret*)

**Margaret** (*changing the subject*) I'll just open these windows, shall I, let some fresh air in. Oh and I'll put these on your desk, shall I? (*The letters*)

*Julia nods and smiles. Margaret collects the letters and puts them on the work table then moves into the conservatory and opens the outer doors*

**Julia** (*steeling herself*) Margaret, please don't misunderstand what I'm going to say but — as soon as I'm mobile again, I really want to be on my own. Need to be on my own. I really don't think I'm going to get better unless I — well — stand on my own two feet. You see, ever since the accident, there's been someone looking after me — first of all Gary and now you and ... anyway. I'm sorry but — that's the way I feel.

*Margaret looks at Julia; during the following she tidies the letters on the work table into a neat pile and pushes the chair neatly under the table*

**Margaret** You don't have to apologize. I understand completely, of course I do. In fact, if we're really honest, it's me who should be making the apologies.

**Julia** Why?

**Margaret** Because ... (*suddenly seeming awkward*) ... because I've been, well, indulging myself, haven't I? Making myself useful because ... because I'm one of these dreadful women who needs to feel useful, it makes me feel, well, important, I suppose, and now that I don't have John ... (*she tries to lighten it*) Poor John ... "You're such a bossy-boots," he used to say, "one of these days you'll organize me into my ... into my grave".

*This moment*

All I hope is that we remain friends.

**Julia** Of course we will. (*She smiles*)

**Margaret** (*returning the smile*) You're quite sure you'll be able to manage tonight?

**Julia** Quite sure.

**Margaret** You know where I am if you need me.

**Julia** I won't need you.

**Margaret** Just let me do one thing and then I'll leave you in peace.

**Julia** What's that?

**Margaret** (*moving into the garden*) Just let me water the garden, it's looking terribly dry — well it hasn't been touched for over a week, has it? — and apart from anything else, I should hate that lovely new shrub to die. It's a Mexican Orange Blossom, isn't it?

*Margaret exits into the unseen part of the garden*

**Julia** What the hell are you on about now? (*She wheels herself across towards the french windows* ) Margaret ! What lovely new ... (*But she stops, having seen the shrub*)

*Margaret enters*

**Margaret** They really are lovely, aren't they? When did you put it in?

**Julia** (*flat, staring out into the garden*) I didn't put it in.

**Margaret** Sorry?

**Julia** I didn't put it in. I've never seen it before.

**Margaret** I'm sorry, I don't ——

**Julia** It wasn't there when I went into hospital. It's Gary — bloody Gary. (*She angrily wheels herself to the telephone and dials*)

**Margaret** (*looking out at the garden and then back at Julia*) I'm sorry but I really don't understand what you're saying.

**Julia** I'm saying that Gary must have been here and done it when I was in hospital. I told him not to touch it, I told him *I'd* do it ... (*Into the receiver*) Oh you're in — good. It's Julia. ... Yes, I've had the operation and I'm back home and I'm fine, thank-you-very-much — just listen to me, will you, Gary? I want to see you. Now. Here. ... No I'm sorry, Gary, I don't care how busy you are, I want to see you — now, right now, or you're in a great deal of trouble. (*She angrily replaces the receiver. To Margaret, clearly distressed*) I told him I didn't want him here any more — I told him.

**Margaret** But why would he — do something like that?

**Julia** I've no idea; presumably he sees it as some sort of welcome home present that'll put him back in credit — well, he's got another think coming, I can tell you.

**Margaret** But ... how did he get in here?

**Julia** He's got a *key*, how many more times?

**Margaret** You mean you didn't get it back from him.

**Julia** That's right. I forgot to get it back from him. (*She's well-aware of how stupid that sounds*)

**Margaret** Well, surely, if all he's done is to ——

**Julia** It isn't all he's done. Something's just clicked, something that was bugging me all the time I was in hospital. The chain was off the door.
**Margaret** Chain? What chain?

*A moment*

**Julia** The morning I left here to go into hospital ... the chain was off the door. Someone had gone out of this house and to do that, they had to take the chain off the door.

*A moment*

**Margaret** (*taking this in*) But why would someone ——
**Julia** Gary, it was Gary.
**Margaret** Why would Gary risk being in the house when you came back?
**Julia** It was a Wednesday. He knows I have a regular meeting with the agency on a Wednesday. It just so happens that this particular Wednesday I cut it short and came home much earlier than I should have done. Otherwise he could have been in and out, doing God knows what, and I would never have known.

*This moment. It is broken by the sound of the doorbell*

**Julia** Let him in, will you, please?
**Margaret** Are you sure you want him to know I'm here? If he feels about me the way you say he does, won't it make things worse?
**Julia** I don't care what he thinks, Margaret: let him in — please.

*A moment*

*Margaret moves to the front door and opens it*

*Gary is outside. He's somewhat surprised to see Margaret*

**Margaret** (*making an attempt at normality*) Hallo, I'm Mrs Haddrell: would you like to go through, please?

*A moment. Then Gary moves uneasily into the room. Margaret closes the door and moves in after him, during the following*

**Gary** (*apprehensive, but trying to sound light*) What's happened, what's it all about?
**Julia** (*coldly*) I told you not to come here, didn't I? I told you I didn't want you in this house so what were you doing here?

*Gary looks from Julia to Margaret who looks decidedly embarrassed*

**Margaret** (*quietly*) Excuse me ...

*She exits into the kitchen*

**Julia** What were you doing here? Stealing something? Or sorting through my underwear again? Just what is it you're playing at, Gary? One minute stealing from me, next minute putting stupid bloody plants in the garden: you're sick, Gary, go and see someone — and leave me alone!

*Gary is stunned and confused. He looks from Julia towards the kitchen, as though for support, but then recovers*

**Gary** Now wait a minute — you can't accuse me of ...
**Julia** (*calling*) Margaret ! (*She holds out a hand*) Give me the key.

*Margaret enters and stays near the kitchen door during the following*

**Gary** (*angrily*) What key?
**Julia** The key — my key — give it to me.
**Gary** I've already given it to you!
**Julia** Liar!
**Gary** (*trying for calm*) All right. All right. The last time I was here, if you remember, you were dashing off to one of your meetings and you could hardly bring yourself to talk to me. You didn't even say goodbye properly. I put the key where you always used to keep it. Behind the books. And I left you a note, here, right here, on the table, telling you what I'd done.
**Julia** I didn't see any note.
**Gary** I left the key and I left a note. Now if you don't mind — I think you've said enough. (*He turns to go*)
**Julia** Wait a minute.

*Gary stops and turns. Julia looks at him, then wheels herself across to the bookshelves and levers herself out of the chair. Margaret moves to help her*

I'm all right, I'm all right. (*She pushes books out of the way, looking for the key*)

*Margaret looks awkwardly at Gary*

*Julia finds the key and turns*

**Gary** All right? Satisfied?

*Finding the key has taken the wind from Julia's sails; she rallies, however*

**Julia** You could have had a copy made.
**Gary** It's a Banham. They won't make a copy unless you've got the owner's certificate. You know that: you told me you had all that trouble before. Anything else?

*This moment*

**Julia** (*quietly*) I'm warning you, Gary ... don't come to this house ever again or I'll send for the police.
**Gary** And I'm warning *you* (*to Margaret*) — and you're my witness — accuse me of one more thing and it's me who'll be sending for the Old Bill — because I tell you this: I really used to like you but you know what I think now? I think it's *you* who's sick, not me — because when it comes to putting stupid bloody plants in the garden, you probably did it yourself. Gawd knows why but it wouldn't be the first time you've done something and then pointed the finger at me, would it, Julia? Would it, Miss Darrow? (*He holds his angry, hurt look then turns to Margaret*) You'd better see me out, make sure I don't pinch none of the silverware. (*He moves to the front door*)

*Margaret glances awkwardly at Julia and then goes after Gary*

*Julia sits in the wheelchair, looking at the key*

(*To Margaret*) You're looking after her now, are you?
**Margaret** (*awkwardly*) Well — yes — sort of, I suppose.
**Gary** Well I wish you luck. If you're anything like me, you're gonna need it.

*He exits*

*Margaret closes the door and remains standing there for a moment, before moving back into the room, looking at Julia. Julia, in the wheelchair, looking at the key, suddenly seems drained of energy. She raises her head slowly and sees Margaret looking at her*

**Julia** He still could have been here. He could have put that thing in the garden and left the key and — when he went out of the house — just ... just closed the door.
**Margaret** (*sounding very uncertain*) Yes.
**Julia** You don't believe me.

**Margaret** It's just that — when we came back just now, the front door was double-locked. You can only do that with the key. So whoever was in the house last — must have taken the key with them. And if *he* left the key where you found it ... I'm sorry, I don't understand. In fact ... no, I mustn't.
**Julia** Mustn't what, Margaret ?
**Margaret** No, it's none of my ——
**Julia** Mustn't what, Margaret ?

*A moment*

**Margaret** You see — you only *think* he was in the house.
**Julia** (*pointing angrily at the garden*) What's that thing? Do I only think I can see *that*?
**Margaret** No, but — you see — last time I was here you said that you and Gary had talked about putting in a shrub or something to brighten that corner .... I said I thought it was rather late in the season but you said you were going along to the garden centre to ——
**Julia** I didn't say that: I said we'd talked about it but that I wasn't going to do anything about it until next year.

*Margaret gives an unconvincing little nod*

You really don't believe me, do you?
**Margaret** And, you see ... the chain — on the door. You said how stupid you were that you often forget to put it on. I suggested you write a little note to yourself and put it on your mirror so that you ... so that you wouldn't forget. You remember that, surely?

*A moment*

**Julia** (*softly*) No.
**Margaret** (*moving to stand close behind Julia*) You mustn't worry, really you mustn't. With all that's happened, you're probably confused. There's always an answer, you know. That's something John was always saying to me: there's always an answer to ——
**Julia** Oh, shut up about bloody John! I'm sick and tired of hearing you going on about ... I'm sorry, I'm really sorry. (*Despite herself, and without looking at Margaret , she holds up her hand*)

*After a moment, Margaret takes Julia's hand and holds it. This moment: the two women holding hands, each looking out at the garden*

**Margaret** D'you know what I think would be a good idea? If you had a nice early night. Would you like that? I'll make you a nice light supper and then you can have a nice early night. And I'll stay with you until you're asleep. Or would you prefer me to stay? I'd be quite happy to. Really. Whatever you want. It's up to you.

*We hold this moment: the two women holding hands*

*Music plays: Billie Holliday singing "Love for Sale"*

*Black-out*

*Margaret exits to the kitchen*

*A bottle of wine and a single flower in a stem vase are set on the coffee table*

*The Lights come up and the music fades on the house speakers, now coming only from the CD player on stage.*

*It is evening. Julia sits on the sofa, fingering a glass of wine*

*Margaret enters from the kitchen, carrying a tray bearing a bowl of soup, a slice of bread on a sideplate and a napkin. She puts the tray on the coffee table, takes up the napkin and puts it on Julia's lap, then passes her the soup, then the spoon*

**Margaret** There.
**Julia** (*stiffly*) Thank you.

*Margaret stands watching like a mother with an adored child. Julia takes a spoonful of soup*

**Margaret** Good?
**Julia** Very.

*A moment: Julia drinking the soup, Margaret watching*

**Margaret** Are you sure that's all you want?
**Julia** What about you?
**Margaret** I'll have something when I get home. (*She sits in the small chair*)

*A moment*

You're seeing the physio tomorrow, aren't you?
**Julia** Tomorrow morning.
**Margaret** What time?

**Julia** Half-eleven I think. Yes. Half-eleven.
**Margaret** I'll be here about quarter to.
**Julia** No, honestly, I can get a cab.
**Margaret** Of course you won't get a cab — I'll be here at quarter to eleven.

*A moment: Julia toying with the soup, Margaret watching her. Then, unable to sit still, Margaret gets up, moves to the CD player and peers at the switches*

**Julia** What are you doing?
**Margaret** (*lightly*) You don't want to listen to this, do you?
**Julia** Yes, I do want to listen to it, that's why I put it on.
**Margaret** But it's so depressing.
**Julia** That's what I like about it. I feel depressed.
**Margaret** Then wouldn't it be better to put on something — cheerful?
**Julia** No, because I'm not feeling cheerful.
**Margaret** But wouldn't cheerful music cheer you up? That's what I do: when I'm feeling down ——
**Julia** You put on your Rodgers and Hammerstein, yes I'm sure you do, but I'm not you, you see, Margaret, I'm me; now please, if you don't mind, I'd like to listen to it.

*This moment. Margaret takes up the CD cover and looks at the picture of Ms Holliday, wrinkles her nose disdainfully and sits again. Julia doesn't look at her, toying with her spoon*

**Margaret** Is it something you'd like to talk about?
**Julia** What?
**Margaret** Why you're depressed.
**Julia** I'm depressed because of *me*, Margaret. I'm depressed because … it doesn't matter. (*She puts down the spoon*) I'm sorry, I'm — I'm really not hungry.
**Margaret** Just another spoonful.

*A moment. Julia takes another mouthful of the soup*

There. (*She collects the plate and tray*) Would you like some fruit?
**Julia** No. Nothing. Thank you.
**Margaret** How can you expect to get better if you ——
**Julia** For God's sake, Margaret!

*This moment. Julia takes a mouthful of wine and sits looking straight ahead. Margaret puts everything other than the bottle of wine on the tray. She takes up the bottle*

Not that.

*A moment. A mini-battle of wills*

*Margaret sets down the bottle and exits into the kitchen with the tray*

*Julia pointedly tops up her glass*

*Margaret enters. She hovers awkwardly for a moment*

**Margaret** Well, I'll ... ummm ... I'll just do the washing up and then I'll be on my way.
**Julia** I'll do the washing up, all right? I'll do it.

*This moment*

**Margaret** You're angry with me, aren't you?
**Julia** (*stiffly*) Why should I be angry with you?
**Margaret** The way I — the way I fuss, I suppose.
**Julia** No I'm not angry with you, I'm just ... you see, what I don't understand, Margaret , is — well, how long has he been dead? Just a few months and yet, somehow, listening to you, watching the way you behave, it's as though — it's as though it never happened, you just don't seem ... (*She trails off*)
**Margaret** You think I don't grieve for him.
**Julia** I know you grieve for him.
**Margaret** But I don't show my grief in the way you think I should show it.
**Julia** What I'm trying to say is ... you seem — you seem more concerned about me than you do about him. I — I just don't understand that.

*This moment*

**Margaret** It would have been very easy for me to give in to what I really feel. But that would have been weakness and I owe it to him, I owe it to John, to be stronger. I know that's what he wants, I know that's what he expects of me. And, you see, by thinking of someone other than myself, by thinking of you, by caring about you, I find that strength. I find a certain — peace of mind, if you like. So that when I said before that, by coming here, I was quite shamelessly indulging myself, what I really wanted to say was that I was — that I am — protecting myself, that if I didn't come here ... that if there wasn't you .... (*For a moment it looks as though she might break down*) Please. Don't let's quarrel. (*She holds out a hand*)

*A moment, and Julia takes Margaret's hand. This moment*

(*Breaking away*) Right. I'm away. Oh — and back to Miss Bossy-Boots again — don't forget to take your pills.

**Julia**  No.
**Margaret**  You really should take them now.
**Julia**  You're absolutely right.
**Margaret**  Where are they?
**Julia**  In the bedroom.

*Margaret makes to move*

I'll get them. (*She gets to her feet, reaching for the crutches*)

*Margaret makes to help her*

I'm all right, really, I'm all right. (*She adjusts the crutches*) I am now going into the bedroom. I may be gone some time. (*She gives a flat smile and begins the slow journey towards the bedroom*)

*Margaret watches Julia go until she is in the hallway, then moves and very deliberately turns off the music. Julia stops and turns*

*Margaret takes up the bottle of wine and exits into the kitchen*

*Black-out*

*Margaret enters*

*A glass of water and bottle of pills are set*

*The Lights come up. It is morning. Julia is standing, leaning somewhat heavily on the telephone chest. Margaret stands by the small chair, holding the crutches*

**Margaret**  One more time.
**Julia**  I don't think I can.
**Margaret**  Of course you can. Come on. For me.

*A moment. Then Julia straightens up, and begins walking, without the crutches, towards Margaret. It is effortful, but she manages several steps before grabbing the back of the sofa*

There you are, you see, you did it — bravo!
**Julia**  Sally Gunnell eat your heart out.
**Margaret**  Another couple of weeks and you can throw these things away forever. Sit down and I'll give you a massage.

*A moment. Julia sits on the sofa. Margaret moves the small chair closer, sits, lifts Julia's leg and gently massages the ankle and calf during the following*

I've been for another interview.

**Julia** And? (*Her eyes close during the following*)

**Margaret** "We'll let you know, Mrs Haddrell."

**Julia** I thought they needed experienced nursing staff.

**Margaret** It's whether they need them of my age, though, isn't it?

**Julia** You make yourself sound like an old woman.

**Margaret** Well — fifty. Fifty-one next October.

**Julia** There you are then — nothing.

**Margaret** Easy to say if you're — what — thirty?

**Julia** I wish. Thirty-four. Now that *is* old.

*Margaret massages for a moment*

**Margaret** It's how you're — perceived, isn't it? Unfortunately, someone in my position is so often made to *feel* like an old woman.

**Julia** That isn't true, surely? Not nowadays.

**Margaret** Don't misunderstand me — I'm not talking in terms of actual physical age, I'm talking in terms of — usefulness. Of — desirability, I suppose you could say. "Well past her sell-by date." Isn't that the revolting expression they use nowadays? About some of us, anyway. Not all of us. But some of us. How many husbands betray their wives because they no longer — measure up ... because they present a mirror-image of his own mortality and so he gets frightened and plays Peter Pan with some willing little tart half as old and twice as cunning.

**Julia** (*opening her eyes*) That's fine — thanks.

*Margaret gives a final little rub, gets up and replaces the chair, looks at her watch and takes up the glass of water and bottle of capsules*

**Margaret** Time for your pills. (*She holds out the capsules*)

*A moment. Julia takes the capsules and swallows them down with the water. As she does so, Margaret unnecessarily tidies the bookshelves*

Is it tomorrow you see your counsellor?

**Julia** Tomorrow morning, yes.

**Margaret** And you'd rather I wasn't here.

**Julia** If you don't mind.

**Margaret** Of course I don't mind. Why should I mind? (*She sees the car blanket over the back of the sofa and moves to tidy it unnecessarily*)

Although if I'm very honest I don't see why you need her: you're just as well-off talking to a sympathetic friend, surely? In my opinion that sort of person does more harm than good. Who gives them the right to tell you how to run your life? If you ask me it's more job creation than a social service.

**Julia** (*wearily*) I'm not asking you, Margaret .

**Margaret** You should have seen the so-called counsellor who turned up on *my* doorstep: some dreadful creature with a second-class degree and an earring in its nose telling *me* how to cope with death — she soon got a flea in her ear, I can tell you.

**Julia** Yes. You said.

**Margaret** Am I boring you? I'm so sorry. (*She sits in the small chair, tight-lipped, prissy, plucking imaginary fluff from her skirt*)

*This moment*

**Julia** Margaret … you haven't touched the answering machine, have you?

**Margaret** Touched the what?

**Julia** The answering machine.

**Margaret** No. Should I have?

**Julia** It's just that — a couple of people have phoned and said they've left messages but there's nothing on the machine.

**Margaret** Perhaps it's not working.

*A moment. Then — clearly for something to do — Margaret gets up, collects the glass and exits into the kitchen*

*Julia remains, sitting alone*

*Black-out*

*Anne enters with her bag and sits on the sofa. Julia sits in the wheelchair*

*The Lights come up. It is the next day. Late morning*

**Anne** You said you might go away or something.

**Julia** Did I?

**Anne** Before you went into hospital you said you might go away to — "break the spell".

**Julia** Oh yes. So I did.

**Anne** It might be a good idea.

**Julia** Yes. Well. We'll see. (*She rubs the bridge of her nose wearily*)

**Anne** And you haven't been tempted to tell her about you and her husband?

**Julia** Tempted, yes. The more she — fusses around me, the more tempted I am. (*A moment*) Every time she comes here I try to say that's it, enough,

but somehow — somehow the moment gets deflected and — I don't seem
to have the energy to pursue it.

**Anne**  And she does look after you.

*This moment*

**Julia**  Yes, she does look after me.

**Anne**  Which can't be all bad. Now that you've dispensed with Gary.

**Julia**  No.

**Anne**  Why did you?

**Julia**  Why did I what?

**Anne**  Get rid of him.

**Julia**  He was stealing from me. And — other things.

**Anne**  That wasn't the reason you gave him.

**Julia**  No, it wasn't. I knew he'd been stealing from me but I couldn't actually
... I'm as much to blame as he is. Truth is, I suppose, he fancied me and
I — well, I let him misread the signals. Let someone get too close and
there's always a price to ... (*Then she realizes what Anne has said*) How do
*you* know what I said to him?

*This moment*

**Anne**  He told me. The afternoon I came here and you'd ——

**Julia**  He did what?

**Anne**  I didn't ask him to, he ——

**Julia**  Why? What the hell's it got to do with you?

**Anne**  He's — concerned about you. He thinks you're very ——

**Julia**  I don't care what he thinks, he's an odd job man, not a bloody
psychologist. That's all I need, the pair of you picking over the bones. Well,
I'd be grateful if you'd stop it. Now, d'you mind — I've got work to do.
(*She levers herself out of the chair, takes up the crutches and moves
determinedly to sit at the drawing board in the conservatory, her back to
us*)

*Anne remains sitting for a moment, then stands, taking up her bag*

**Anne**  I'll telephone you.

**Julia**  Perhaps you shouldn't bother.

**Anne**  I'll telephone you.

*This moment*

   *Anne exits*

*Julia slowly and silently begins to cry. She puts her hands to her head*

*Black-out*

*Margaret enters*

*The Lights come up. It is evening. Margaret is encouraging Julia to walk without the crutches. Julia tries, gives up and collapses into the sofa. Margaret tidies the crutches against the end of the sofa during the following*

**Julia** I'm sorry. I'm just so tired.
**Margaret** Did you not sleep again?
**Julia** I don't sleep at night and I'm half-asleep all day. I don't understand it, I seem to be getting weaker instead of stronger. I don't seem able to concentrate on anything. God knows when I'll get down to some work again. (*She lies on the sofa*) I lost another job yesterday. I just didn't have the energy to say yes.
**Margaret** Have you spoken to the doctor?
**Julia** What will he say? The same as last time: "Keep taking the pills".
**Margaret** He is right, of course.

*A moment. Margaret starts to tidy Julia's work table*

**Julia** What are you doing?
**Margaret** I thought I'd tidy your ——
**Julia** It doesn't need tidying.
**Margaret** But it's so — messy.
**Julia** I like it messy. I only know where things are when I can't find them. Please. Don't touch it.

*This moment. Margaret takes up the bottle of capsules from the work table. She moves towards Julia, unscrewing the lid; she tips out the capsules and shake them in her hand, during the following*

**Margaret** You are taking the prescribed amount?
**Julia** Yes, nurse: just like it says on the bottle.
**Margaret** There seem to be fewer here than there should be.
**Julia** I take them — when it says I should take them. (*Her eyes close*)
**Margaret** (*returning the capsules to the bottle and putting the bottle on the table*) Because ... do you remember I said — when you were worried about — well — forgetting things — I said ——
**Julia** "Don't worry", you said, "there's always a reason". There, you see, I remembered *that*, didn't I? (*She gives a flat smile*)
**Margaret** The reason might be ... in my experience, medication of the strength you've been given — unless taken exactly as and when prescribed — can have — well — side effects.

**Julia** How d'you mean — side effects?

**Margaret** Dizziness — loss of energy — sleepiness — hallucination even. What I'm saying is ... taken incorrectly, it could account for your — confusion about — certain things.

*A moment as Julia takes this in*

(*Brightly*) Perhaps it might be an idea for us to get a little pill box or something and put in a day's ration at a time — what d'you think?

*This moment*

**Julia** Whatever you say.

*A moment. Julia's eyes are fully closed now; she is falling asleep. A moment. Margaret moves until she is standing directly behind the sleeping Julia. She stands looking down at her, nothing in her face*

*Black-out*

*Margaret exits*

*Julia remains on the sofa and wraps herself in the car blanket. A bottle of pills with a note propped against it is set on the coffee table*

*The Lights come up. It is late evening. The hall light and a side light are on. Julia is asleep. A moment*

*Julia wakens with a start as if from an uneasy dream, jerking her head round, not knowing where she is. She calms, looks at her watch — "God, have I slept that long?" — sits a moment and sees a note propped up against a bottle of pills on the coffee table. She takes up the note, knowing what it will say ("Don't forget to take your pills"), reads it quickly, screws it up and tosses it at the waste basket. She makes to stand, but snatches up the pill bottle*

I'm taking them, all right? I'm taking them.

*She stands, stuffing the bottle into a pocket, takes up the crutches and moves to check that the conservatory windows are locked, turns off the side light, moves into the hall, almost goes into the bedroom but remembers and puts the chain on the front door, then turns*

Good-night house.

*She turns off the hall light and exits into the bedroom*

*A moment. Then the shaft of light from the upstairs window falls on to the
conservatory roof and a moment later the upstairs door opens; the undefined
shadow is framed by the shaft of light coming down the stairs*

*Black-out*

*Anne enters, wearing her top coat, and sits on the sofa*

*The Lights come up. It is late morning. Anne looks uneasy*

*After a moment, Margaret enters from the bedroom, quietly closing the
door after her. She moves into the room. Anne stands on seeing her*

**Margaret** Still fast asleep, I'm afraid.
**Anne** Oh well. No matter. (*She smiles*)
**Margaret** (*returning the smile*) I could wake her if you want me to — I mean
I'd rather not, but ——
**Anne** No, it's — it's OK.

*A moment. We should sense each woman waiting for the other to make the
first move*

**Margaret** I suppose I should introduce myself properly ...
**Anne** No, that's all right: I know who you are, Mrs Haddrell.
**Margaret** Oh. (*She sits, perplexed*)
**Anne** You sound surprised.
**Margaret** Yes, I ... do sit down — please.

*Anne sits in the small chair and Margaret sits on the sofa*

Yes you see ... I knew she was seeing you and I assumed she would have
told you about me but when it came up in conversation she said, no, she
hadn't told you. I must admit I was surprised — I would have thought that
... anyway: I suppose that's why she was to anxious for me to leave. So that
I wouldn't meet you. Another five minutes and I wouldn't have. (*She gives
her "nice little woman" smile*) How much has she said about me?

*A moment as Anne chooses her words*

**Anne** I know that you wrote to her ... I know that she agreed to see you ...
I know that you've been very kind to her and that you've become — well
— friends.

**Margaret** (*smiles*) Yes. Oh yes. Then why on earth would she say she didn't know me?

**Anne** I don't know. Perhaps I should ask her. (*She smiles, making it clear that that's as far as she's going*)

**Margaret** Yes.

*This moment*

**Anne** Mrs Haddrell — at the risk of offending you ——

**Margaret** No — please — I have great respect for people who do your sort of work — please — say whatever you feel you have to say.

**Anne** I ... frankly I think that the relationship is unhealthy for both of you and I can't see that it will resolve anything. In fact I think that in the long run there's the danger that it can only cause pain — to both of you.

**Margaret** I know, I know! Don't you think I've tried to stop it? Don't you think I want to stop it? I'm sorry, that's unfair, why should you know anything about me other than ... other than what she's chosen to tell you. (*She looks towards the bedroom door as though anxious not to be overheard*) Did you know this young man who was looking after her?

**Anne** Gary. Yes.

**Margaret** I don't suppose she told you that I was once a nurse.

**Anne** No. No she didn't.

**Margaret** I happened to tell her that before I was married I was a nurse. And she said ... she said, in that case why do I need Gary? You can look after me. A week later she accused him of stealing money and — other things and — got rid of him.

*A moment*

(*Getting up and looking out of the window*) Since then my life hasn't been my own. She seems to want me to do everything for her. One minute she's calm and — so very very nice — the next minute she's quite — irrational, screaming abuse and accusing me of things I haven't done and — I told her — you need help — not me, proper help, treatment — I try to get her to see a doctor — and she refuses point-blank. I've seen enough doctors, she says, and what have they done for me? Look at me. I suggest that she speak to you and she just ... well, as I say, she becomes quite irrational. I know I should put an end to it, I know I should walk away, for her sake as well as mine but you see ... I'm afraid.

*A moment*

**Anne** Afraid of what, Mrs Haddrell?

*A moment*

**Margaret** (*turning towards Anne*) She said if you don't come here any more
... if you don't help me ... I shall kill myself. I shall kill myself and my
death will be your responsibility and how will you live with that, Mrs
Haddrell?

*This moment*

(*Sitting on the sofa*) What worries me is that I believe she's hoarding her
pills, the painkillers, I've seen her pretend to take them and I know she
hasn't. I've looked everywhere for them but ... God only knows where
she's keeping them.

*This moment*

**Anne**  (*standing*) I'll speak to her GP, see if he can ——
**Margaret**  (*standing*) I've already spoken to him. As I said, she refuses to
have him anywhere near her. But I'll keep trying. I promise you. When will
you come and see her?
**Anne**  That's the problem: I'm away on a course for a few days.
**Margaret**  Oh. I wonder then if it would be best if I don't tell her you were
here. That we met. Perhaps I should say that you telephoned and cancelled
the appointment, because, you see — I don't think I could cope if she
accused me of — interfering. It's so much easier if you're not emotionally
involved and the thing is, you see — I really have grown rather fond of her.
I hope you understand.

*A moment*

**Anne**  (*giving a little nod*) Yes. Yes of course I understand. Tell her I'll be
in touch as soon as I get back. In the meantime I'll brief one of my
colleagues, just in case she needs to see someone urgently.
**Margaret**  Please. I need help.

*This moment*

*Black-out*

*Anne exits; Julia enters and lies down on the sofa under the blanket*

*A small pillbox, a medicine bottle and a Kleenex tissue with several of
Julia's capsules on it, are set on the work table*

*The Lights come up*

*Late afternoon. Julia is asleep under the blanket. Margaret, wearing her glasses and a neat little apron, is sitting at the work table. She is holding up one of the capsules, examining it against the light. Satisfied, she returns most of the capsules to the bottle, and puts four of them into the pillbox. She takes off her glasses, puts them and the bottle into her apron pocket, carefully screws the tissue into a ball and holds it in her hand as she moves to stand looking down at Julia, nothing in her face. Then she bends and none-too-gently shakes Julia's shoulder*

**Julia** (*waking with a start*) I'm sorry, I'm sorry. (*She looks around, still half-asleep*)
**Margaret** It's six o'clock. Wakey-wakey, young lady.

*Margaret exits into the kitchen*

*Julia tries to pull herself into wakefulness*

*Margaret enters with a prepared tray of light food which includes a glass of water and the pillbox*

(*Setting the tray down on the table*) Here we are — all ready — and do try to eat some of it for a change, there seems little point in my bothering otherwise.
**Julia** (*remembering hazily*) What about the doctor, the doctor was coming.
**Margaret** (*plumping cushions*) He came.
**Julia** Why didn't you wake me?
**Margaret** He said it was better to let you sleep.
**Julia** But I sleep all the time.
**Margaret** That's what I told him: she sleeps all day, I said, and then she pretends she can't sleep at night.
**Julia** (*protesting mildly*) I *don't* sleep at night.
**Margaret** Yes — well — you're not alone, are you, dear? (*Giving a tart smile and neatly folding the blanket as:*) Anyway. He said it was perfectly normal. Nature's way of getting your strength back. I told him about your leg and he said that if the pain doesn't get any better he'll have you in for an X-ray early next week. But the main thing is, he wanted me to make sure I told you that you mustn't worry — that, all right, things are being a little slow — but another couple of weeks and you'll be as right as rain, as long as you've got someone like me looking after you. "My God", I said, "I do nothing but look after her". (*She smiles*) And happy to do it. (*She moves towards the kitchen, but stops, seeing the ornament Julia had previously*

*repositioned*) I think this looks better here, don't you? (*She moves the ornament*) Yes. Much better.

*She exits into the kitchen*

*After a moment, Julia takes out two pills and drinks them down with the water*

*Margaret enters, wearing a cardigan in place of the apron, and stands by the doorway, watching Julia, nothing in her face. Then she moves into the room*

*Julia seems not to hear Margaret, her mind miles away*

I've been thinking — when you're feeling brighter — why don't we have a nice night out? We could go to the cinema or the theatre or something — and have a meal. Why don't we do that?

**Julia** (*coming back to the present*) I'm sorry, I ... I didn't hear what you said.

**Margaret** (*taking the glass from Julia*) It doesn't matter. I was talking nonsense anyway. You won't want to go out with me, you'll want to go out with someone of your own age, of course you will. Are you really not going to eat this?

**Julia** I'm sorry.

*Margaret makes it quite clear what she thinks of that, putting the glass on the tray and making to go into the kitchen with it*

I thought Anne might have called.

**Margaret** Anne? Oh, Anne, your counsellor. Were you expecting her to call?

**Julia** I thought she might. Yes.

**Margaret** (*cheerily*) Perhaps she's given you up as a bad job.

**Julia** Probably.

*Margaret exits into the kitchen*

*A moment. Julia tries to stand, but is too weary. She sinks back into the chair*

*Margaret enters*

**Margaret** Oh yes: I asked the doctor to come and see you again tomorrow morning.

*Julia nods*

I'll try to be here, of course I will, but I might have another interview. That's something we ought to talk about: what happens if I do get a position? Who'll look after you? I don't know what sort of friends you've got but I do find it surprising that none of them has so much as telephoned — they must know how poorly you are, surely? (*She sits and twiddles with a cushion*) What really surprises me is — well, to put it bluntly — that you're not married. Or at least that there isn't a man in your life.

**Julia**  Yes, that's pretty blunt, I suppose.

**Margaret**  What I mean is, you're a very attractive young woman. I would have ——

**Julia**  Thank you but even if you're right, the one doesn't necessarily follow from the other.

**Margaret**  Oh dear.

**Julia**  Oh dear what?

**Margaret**  I've obviously said the wrong thing.

**Julia**  Perhaps I always choose the wrong sort of man.

**Margaret**  What sort of man is that?

**Julia**  My sort of man. Perhaps I'm not very good at relationships. Perhaps I don't want a relationship. Perhaps I prefer living on my own. Perhaps I've left it too late to do anything else ... look — I really don't want to talk about it — sorry.

*This moment*

**Margaret**  I completely forgot: I've got something for you. A little present. (*She moves towards the kitchen*)

*Julia runs weary fingers through her hair: not another bloody present*

Close your eyes.

**Julia**  (*sighs*) Margaret ——

**Margaret**  Please. It's a surprise.

*Margaret exits into the kitchen*

*Julia sighs and closes her eyes dutifully*

*After a moment, Margaret enters with an unseen something and goes straight to the CD player*

*We now see that she is holding a CD. She turns on the machine, puts in the CD and starts it. Music plays: a lusty male vocal of "The Surrey With The Fringe On Top"*

*Julia opens her eyes disbelievingly*

(*Beaming at Julia*) There. Rodgers and Hammerstein. Just like you said. That's better, isn't it?

*Margaret turns up the volume and exits into the kitchen*

*The singer sings on*

*Black-out*

*Julia exits*

*The music fades*

*The Lights come up. It is evening. The room is empty. After a moment, the telephone rings*

*Margaret enters from the kitchen and moves quickly to take up the receiver on the small chest*

(*Into the phone; quietly*) Hallo? ... No, she isn't I'm afraid, she's asleep. Margaret, Margaret Haddrell, we've spoken before, I believe. ... Yes, that's right. ... Not too good, I'm afraid. She seems terribly depressed again. ... Didn't she? Well, I did tell her, although quite honestly she doesn't seem to want to speak to anyone, I'm getting quite worried about her.

*During the following, Julia enters from the bedroom, leaning heavily on the crutches, in time at least to see Margaret replacing the receiver*

Let me write down your number again and I'll try to get her to call you. ... 0745. ... Yes, of course I will. Bye. (*Replacing the receiver; to Julia*) Someone trying to sell you double-glazing. I assured him you didn't want any, special offer or no.

*She smiles and exits into the kitchen*

*Julia stands still for a moment and then moves to sit on the sofa, propping the crutches against the arm. She seems exhausted from this exertion*

*Margaret enters, carrying a glass of water. She stands in the archway, watching Julia*

**Julia** (*suddenly becoming aware of Margaret, jerking her head round to see her*) What is it?

**Margaret** What's what?

**Julia** Why are you looking at me?

**Margaret** Looking at you?

**Julia** You were looking at me.

**Margaret** I was bringing you this. (*She indicates the water. She moves in to give the water to Julia and then takes two of the capsules from the pillbox and holds them out for Julia to take*)

**Julia** Margaret — I really would prefer to answer the telephone myself.

**Margaret** I thought you hadn't heard it.

**Julia** Why didn't you call me?

**Margaret** Because as I said, it was someone trying to ——

**Julia** I mean when it rang. Why did you answer it?

**Margaret** I did call you. Of course I did. Why wouldn't I? Now please. (*She holds out the capsules*)

*A moment Julia takes the capsules and swallows them down. Margaret watches her, discreetly pocketing the pillbox*

*When Julia has finished, Margaret takes the glass and exits into the kitchen*

*Julia looks edgy*

*Margaret enters in her topcoat*

**Margaret** (*brightly*) Right then. I'm away. I'll see you tomorrow. (*She collects her bag*) Oh, and I must remember to pick up your skirt.

**Julia** What skirt?

**Margaret** Your grey skirt — you asked me to take it to the cleaners. (*Jokily chiding*) Now don't say you've forgotten that, it was only yesterday morning. (*She kisses the top of Julia's head and heads to the hallway*)

**Julia** Margaret — I'm going away.

*Margaret stops in her tracks*

Tomorrow. I should have told you. Sorry.

**Margaret** Going where?

**Julia** (*patently lying*) A friend of mine has a cottage. In Dorset. She phoned and asked me if I'd like to go down there with her.

**Margaret** (*moving back into the room*) For how long?

**Julia** A week. Two weeks. It doesn't matter, I can ... I can stay as long as I like.

*A moment*

**Margaret** Why didn't you tell me before?

**Julia** I meant to, I — I forgot.

**Margaret** You forgot something as important as that?

**Julia** (*with a slight hint of defiance*) I forget most things — don't I?

*This was a mistake and Julia knows it*

**Margaret** Yes, well in my opinion it's the best thing that could happen.

**Julia** (*relieved*) You don't mind.

**Margaret** (*almost laughing*) Why should I mind?

**Julia** I just thought ——

**Margaret** It's exactly what you need.

**Julia** Yes.

**Margaret** We both need.

**Julia** Yes, that's what I ——

**Margaret** Do you good and give me a rest — a chance to "do my own thing" as they say.

**Julia** (*attempting a smile*) Yes.

**Margaret** Yes. (*She smiles back*) You won't be on your own?

**Julia** No — no, there'll be someone with me.

**Margaret** As long as you're looked after.

**Julia** Yes — yes, I will be.

**Margaret** You promise me.

**Julia** I promise you.

*There is a slight pause*

**Margaret** Good. Good. (*She smiles*) What time are you leaving?

**Julia** Ten o'clock.

**Margaret** I'll help you pack.

**Julia** No. Thanks. My friend will do it.

**Margaret** I'll see you off anyway.

**Julia** No — please.

**Margaret** I know you, young woman — I want to make quite sure you've got all your pills and everything. (*Making it sound light*) Besides — I want to meet this friend of yours and let her know exactly what she's in for.

*Julia makes to protest*

(*Quickly*) No ifs, no buts … I shall be here at half-past nine. Now go to bed early and try to get a good night's sleep. You'll need it if you've got all that travelling tomorrow. (*She smiles, moves into the hallway and opens the door*)

*Julia listens for the sound of the door closing*

*Margaret, instead of going out, closes the door and moves out of sight behind the archway*

*A moment. Then Julia quickly takes up the cordless telephone from the coffee table, dials and waits anxiously. Margaret reappears to stand by the front door, listening*

**Julia** (*into the phone*) Mrs Bennett please, Anne Bennett. ... When will she be back? (*She listens, closing her eyes in quiet despair*) If you tell her that Julia phoned, Julia Darrow, and will she please call me as soon as she's back. Thank you. (*A moment. She re-dials and waits. Then, relieved*) Gary? It's Julia — no, please, please listen to me. I have to see you, Gary, I have to talk to you. As soon as you can — now. Please Gary, please. ... Thank you. Thanks. (*She slowly replaces the receiver*)

*This moment, with Julia sitting holding the telephone, Margaret standing by the door*

*The Lights fade*

*Margaret exits*

*A bottle of red wine and part-filled glass are set on the coffee table and the cordless telephone on the work table. The chain is on the door*

*The Lights come up. It is an hour or so later. Julia stands by the stairs, waiting anxiously. After a moment, the doorbell rings. Even though she has been waiting for it, the sound makes Julia start*

**Julia**  Is that you, Gary?

*Gary is outside the front door*

**Gary**  (*off*) What d'you want?
**Julia**  (*opening the door slightly*) Come inside. (*Satisfied that it is Gary, she takes the chain off the door*)
**Gary**  (*off, not coming in*) Oh yeah? Last time I was in this house ——
**Julia**  Please, Gary.

*A moment. Gary comes in, avoiding looking at Julia. She closes the door*

Go through. Please.

*A moment. Gary moves into the room, looking around suspiciously. Julia follows him slowly, using the crutches*

**Gary** (*turning to look at Julia*) What's wrong, you look terrible.

**Julia** (*sitting wearily*) I have to talk to you, Gary.

**Gary** I think you said enough last time, don't you?

**Julia** I know you're angry with me, you've got every right to be angry with me but ... please; I need your help.

*This moment*

**Gary** What sort of help?

**Julia** I don't want to be left on my own with her.

**Gary** Whaddya talking about?

**Julia** I don't want to be left on my own with her, please don't leave me on my own with her.

**Gary** Are you talking about your friend?

**Julia** (*confused, rambling*) She's not a friend, I know she isn't, she's not a friend ... you see, she says she's looking after me but all the time she's doing things, saying things — and she's got rid of all my real friends. She says they don't telephone me any more but they do, I know they do. She's lying to me, Gary, I know she is, she's lying to me and she's taking control of my life, that's what she's doing, you see, she's taking control of me and I know why, Gary — she *knows*. Somehow she knows and she's trying to punish me.

**Gary** (*not following*) She knows what?

*Julia looks at Gary, then shakes her head. This moment*

Whaddya want *me* to do?

**Julia** I want you to come here again.

**Gary** How d'you mean, come here?

**Julia** I want it to be like it was before.

**Gary** You want me to work for you again?

**Julia** As soon as you can. Tomorrow. Tomorrow morning.

**Gary** You give me the elbow and then you expect me to ——

**Julia** She's coming here, you see. I told her not to but she'll come here, I know she will and I don't want to be on my own with her any more.

*This moment*

**Gary** I'll think about it.

**Julia** Gary ——

**Gary** What do you expect me to say? I have to stand here listening to all that stuff about her — what was it? — taking you over and all I can think of is that's exactly what you said about me. Didn't you? And I know, I know,

I wasn't doing all those things you accused me of doing, so why should I believe ... Truth is, coupla months ago I would have been back here like a shot but not now, Jules, not now. I've learned my lesson. See ... I think you get the wrong idea about people who try to help you. I think it's you who needs to — hurt people. Sorry.

*This moment. Gary moves towards the hallway, then turns to look at Julia*

Tell you what I'll do: I'll come here tomorrow morning, just to see if you're all right. OK?

*This moment. She gives a grateful little nod. A moment*

Good-night, Jules. (*He again makes to go*)
**Julia** Gary ... take the key.
**Gary** Not on your life.

*He exits*

*Julia remains sitting. Then, using the crutches, she moves to put the chain back on the door and then moves as quickly as she can to put the locks on the garden door*

*Margaret comes quietly down the stairs with her handbag. She takes the chain off the door, opens the door and then shuts it noisily*

*Julia gasps and jerks round to see her*

**Margaret** Sorry — did I frighten you?
**Julia** What are you doing here?
**Margaret** I got half-way home and realized I'd left my purse. I think I might have left it in the kitchen.

*She exits into the kitchen and enters, holding up the purse, which she puts into her handbag during the following*

Thank goodness for that: I don't know what I would have done if ——
**Julia** How did you get in?
**Margaret** How did I what? Oh, yes, sorry, I should have said — no wonder you look like you've seen a ghost — I was just about to knock when I noticed that the door wasn't properly shut. He must have left it open — your young man, what's-his-name, Gary. That was him I saw, was it?

*A moment*

**Julia** Yes. (*She sits on the sofa*)

**Margaret** What was he doing here? He wasn't causing trouble, was he?

**Julia** No, he just came to see me.

**Margaret** He just knocked on your door and you let him in — after all you've said to me about him? You do surprise me. (*She takes the pillbox from her bag*)

*Julia does not see the pillbox*

**Julia** Margaret, I'm sorry but I have to go to bed — I'm tired and ——

**Margaret** You have a long journey tomorrow. Yes. I know. (*She holds out the pillbox*) Let me see you take these and I'll go.

**Julia** I've already taken them.

**Margaret** I don't think so. (*She opens the box* ) You *said* you were going to take them but you can't have because there are still four here, that's why we put them in this box, wasn't it, so that we'd know exactly how many you've taken. (*She takes out two of the capsules and holds them out to Julia*)

**Julia** I know I've taken them.

**Margaret** And I know you haven't and I shall stay here until you have because otherwise ——

**Julia** All right. All right. (*She holds out her hand*)

*Margaret gives Julia the capsules. Julia takes up the glass of wine and swallows the capsules, her hands shaking*

Now will you please go, Margaret .

**Margaret** Just like that?

**Julia** Margaret ——

**Margaret** That's all the thanks I get, is it? "Now will you please go, Margaret?"

**Julia** I want you to go.

**Margaret** Show me to the door then.

*Julia looks at her*

I want to make sure you lock it properly this time, I want to make sure you put the chain on; if you don't put the chain on, anyone can walk in, can't they? And we know all about that, don't we? We get all sorts of goings-on, all sorts of accusations. Besides, it's only polite, isn't it? People leave and you show them to the door.

*This moment. Then Julia pulls herself out of the sofa and reaches for the crutches*

(*Taking the crutches out of Julia's reach*) You don't need these, you know you don't. All right then, perhaps you do. Well here they are. Come and get them. (*She stands, holding out the crutches, smiling*)

*This moment. Julia is putting off what she now knows must be the moment of confrontation. She takes a couple of painful steps*

There you are, you see — good girl!

*Julia takes another couple of steps, but her strength has gone. She grips the back of the sofa and slides into it*

**Margaret** No? Oh dear. Well I tell you what ... I'll leave them here and you can try again. (*She hurls the crutches into the hallway*) You're a liar, aren't you — "Jules?" He was here because you asked him to come here ——
**Julia** You know, don't you?
**Margaret** Of course I know, I've just said.
**Julia** You know about John and me.
**Margaret** John and you? What about John and you, what should I know about John and you?
**Julia** You know!

*This moment*

**Margaret** You'd been "seeing" him for about three months, hadn't you? Hadn't you?
**Julia** (*softly*) Yes.
**Margaret** About three months. Yes. I knew of course. Not that it was you. That it was someone. I always knew when he was betraying me. He was such a poor liar. You would have thought he'd be something of an expert, he'd done it so often. Lied to me. Betrayed me. Did you think you were the first, did you think you were special? Good God no. It would take the many fingers of many hands to count his — waywardness, his ability to — sniff out a bitch on heat. In the early days I used to — go for his throat but over the years I learned to close my eyes, to pretend I was unaware, because I knew it was just a game with him, a fix — is that the word? — yes, a fix he needed. And because he was always discreet and because I loved him and because he always came home to where he belonged. He loved *me*, you see: I was the only one of consequence.
**Julia** What do you want me to say, that I'm sorry? Well I am, I'm sorry, I'm truly sorry, I didn't want it to happen ...
**Margaret** Didn't want it to happen? You knew he was married, didn't you? You knew he had a wife.

**Julia** It was wrong — all right? It was wrong.

**Margaret** Pity you didn't think of that then. But then, what *do* you think of, other than yourself?

**Julia** You were his responsibility. Not mine.

**Margaret** Oh. I see.

**Julia** It was an affair.

**Margaret** Sex.

**Julia** Yes — all right — sex. Nothing else.

**Margaret** And that was all right with you, was it? That's all you wanted from him?

**Julia** Yes! (*But*) I knew it wasn't going anywhere, I didn't want it to go anywhere and neither did he. For God's sake, Margaret, you said it yourself — I was just one of his ——

**Margaret** No. This time it was different. This time he didn't come home. Did he?

*This moment*

**Julia** (*feeling the icy chill of real fear; trying to remain as calm as possible*) Why did you come here, Margaret? What is it you want from me?

*Margaret looks at Julia and takes up her handbag, moves to the work table and takes various items from the bag during the following, indicating them as they are mentioned*

**Margaret** Someone dies and the next-of-kin has a great deal of clearing up to do: bills to be paid, letters to be answered, credit cards to be settled. For example, on the night he died: a double room at the Chapel Park Hotel, booked in advance on Visa, not used but still to be paid for. Once it became clear to me that you were the current object of his desire, I began to build up quite a little picture of dinners here, hotel nights there, the odd little trinket even. He was always very generous, wasn't he? Appreciative of services rendered. (*She "smiles"*) The day after he died I had a telephone call from the police to say that although I couldn't have the body — it could not be "released for burial" until after the inquest — I could have the belongings; the clothing he was wearing that night, the contents of his pockets, wallet, money, keys, all the usual. Well, not quite all the usual. There was a key I'd never seen before. This key. (*She holds up a Banham key*)

**Julia** You've had a key to this house. All this time, you've had a key to this house.

**Margaret** I came here one afternoon, on impulse, and yes, as I thought, as I hoped even, the key fitted. When you were first in hospital I came here time and time again. To inspect your little love nest. To see what sort of woman had taken my husband away from me. What sort of woman I had to deal with. And how.

*Julia looks at Margaret, then, making a huge effort, gets out of the chair and drags herself slowly, painfully, towards the cordless telephone*

**Margaret**  Where d'you think you're going?
**Julia**  I'm phoning the police, I'm phoning the police.
**Margaret**  Please … let *me* do it. After all, I've done everything else for you.(*She goes to the other telephone, takes it up as though to dial but then pulls the cord from the socket and violently sweeps the telephone to the floor*)
**Julia**  (*leaning on a chair, breathing heavily*) What are you going to do?
**Margaret**  What am I going to do? I'm going to punish you. I'm going to pay you back, not just you — for all of them, for all those years the likes of you have been humiliating me. Taking what was mine. Do sit down. You look so tired. Are you still not sleeping? All those pills you take and you're still not sleeping. Guilty conscience perhaps? Guilty conscience? You, surely not? Something else, something quite different. Shall I tell you? Yes, of course I shall, I want you to know everything's that happening to you … Better if you sit down, I think. Sit down.

*A moment. Julia sits. Margaret moves to the work table, takes up the pillbox and takes out one of the capsules, demonstrating what she says*

I've been very naughty. I changed your sleeping pills for something quite unsuitable. It's very easy to do: you just carefully take them apart, tip out the contents and replace it with whatever. In this case, indigestion powder. And the reason that you've been getting so much pain with your leg is because I did exactly the same thing with your painkillers — what you've been taking is the contents of the sleeping tablets, which is why you're so drowsy most of the time, so disorientated. (*She moves to the sofa to look down at Julia* ) Except the ones I gave you just now. They were a cocktail, a very strong cocktail, of the sleeping pills and the painkillers. About, oh, three days' supply. And quite lethal.
**Julia**  You're mad.

*Margaret suddenly seizes Julia's hair, pulling her head right back*

**Margaret**  My husband is dead, I have nothing to live for: why should you be allowed to survive?
**Julia**  His death had nothing to do with me, nothing.

**Margaret** I should have been with him when he died, not you. And for that I hate you. I — hate — you. (*She maintains her grip and then releases it. She moves to sit in the small chair, neatly as ever, knees together*)

*During the following, Julia drags herself towards the work table and the cordless telephone*

As you so rightly say, I came into this house as and when I liked: there were things I had to do, you see — break a vase and replace it, steal money, all those things you accused Gary of. You nearly caught me once. The night before you went into hospital. I was planning a special surprise for you but you came home early. I wouldn't bother with the telephone by the way. I've made sure it doesn't work. For the time being anyway.

*Nevertheless, Julia tries the telephone and finds that Margaret has told the truth; Margaret continues. Julia stands with her back to Margaret, staring down sightlessly at the work table*

Poor Gary. He must be as confused as you were. But I needed to get him out of the way, you see: I needed to have you all to myself. I needed to provide evidence of the imbalance of your mind. I needed to — embroider the picture of the potential suicide. Between Gary and your counsellor, I think I've done it rather well, and, let's face it, you do have a history, don't you? I do wish you'd sit down. You'll only fall down. More clearing up for me to do. (*She looks at her watch*) I'd say you've got about twenty minutes. And then sleep and then ... Would you like some music while you're waiting? Yes, you like music, don't you? Let's see if we can find you some — music to die by. (*She turns her back on Julia and looks through the collection of CDs*)

*Julia turns, and we see that she is holding the scissors. She moves painfully slowly towards Margaret*

(*Unaware of Julia*) Now what have we got here? No, no, far too morbid. How about this? No, no I don't think so. Ah! Now this is absolutely right, this is perfect. (*She turns on the machine and inserts a CD. It begins to play: Nat King Cole singing "It's Only a Paper Moon"*) There. (*She turns, smiling*)

*Julia, near Margaret, raises the scissors as though to plunge them into Margaret. Margaret slowly smiles, pulling back her collar, offering her bare neck as the target*

Do it ... do it.

*But Julia seems frozen. This moment. Then Margaret unhurriedly takes Julia's wrist and slowly forces her backwards so that she falls on to the sofa. Margaret twists the scissors from Julia's hand and stands over Julia with the scissors at her throat. Quite suddenly she withdraws the scissors, pats the blanket straight and moves away to return the scissors to the work table*

Now then. I have some clearing up to do. Can't have the place looking untidy when they find you, can we?

*During the following, and as though nothing untoward has happened, Margaret moves to take up the telephone and plug it back in. She then collects the crutches and leans them against the sofa, takes the pills out of her handbag and scatters them on the coffee table, then roughly pulls Julia upright so that she is sitting. She then turns off the CD player*

**Julia** (*scarcely audible*) They'll know.
**Margaret** I beg your pardon?
**Julia** They'll know: they'll know it was you.
**Margaret** D'you think so? Well — we'll have to wait and see won't we? Or at least I will. (*She smiles, then stands behind the sofa and pats a cushion*) I've had a practice run, you see. Oh, many years ago now. I did tell you he was engaged when I first met him, didn't I? She wouldn't have been any good to him, she was a pallid little creature, always ill, I never did know what he saw in her. That was how I met him, I was looking after her. I loved him from the minute I saw him. She had to go, didn't she? He needed someone to look after him properly. And I did, you know, I really did.

*This moment, with Julia sitting, staring, trying to keep her eyes open, Margaret standing behind her*

He was a wonderful husband, you know. Wonderful.

*This moment*

*Black-out*

*Anne and Gary enter. Gary stands* L, *Anne* R; *Margaret moves* C

**Coroner's Voice** Ladies and gentlemen: as members of a Coroner's Jury, it is your duty to consider and decide how Julia Darrow died and the cause of her death rather than to indicate the identity of any person or persons you might believe to be implicated in her demise ——

*The last part of this speech is overlapped by the first sentence of Gary's speech as a spot comes up on him,* L

**Gary** — she asked me to stay with her but because — because of all the trouble there was before, I didn't. I wish I had but I didn't. I come round the next morning like I said I would ——

*The last sentence of this speech is overlapped by the first sentence of Anne's speech as a spot comes up on her,* R

**Anne** — she was deeply depressed by what had happened to her. The tragedy was, I'd only been out of the office for half an hour when she phoned. Otherwise — otherwise I might have been able to help her. If she'd let me — our relationship had deteriorated considerably since ——

*The last sentence of this speech is overlapped by the first sentence of Margaret's speech as a spot comes up on her,* C

**Margaret** — I left the house just before seven. She seemed much the same as usual except — except that just before I left, she said to me, "I'm sorry". I asked her what for and she said, "It doesn't matter — as long as you know I'm sorry". I wish I could have done more for her. She had so much to live for.

*This moment. The Lights fade on Anne and Gary so that we are left with Margaret. The Light slowly tightens on her. There is the merest trace of a smile on her mouth*

*Music plays: Billie Holliday singing "Love for Sale"*

*The Light on Margaret fades slowly to Black-out*

CURTAIN

# FURNITURE AND PROPERTY LIST

## ACT I

*On stage*:    Antique umbrella stand
Chesterfield sofa. *On it*: scatter cushions, folded car blanket
Small buttonback chair
Coffee table. *On it*: small pile of magazines
Shelves. *On them*: books, ornaments, CD player, CDs, piles of
    magazines
Small occasional table. *On it*: ornaments and plants
Small antique chest of drawers. *On it*: table lamp, telephone, answering
    machine. *In second drawer*: two five pound notes
Drawing board
Draughtsman's chair
Plan rolls
Battered, medium-sized portfolio
Potted plants
Two tables. *On them*: laptop computer, papers, opened envelope, card,
    Swan Morton cutting knife, pencils, pens, large paper scissors,
    cordless telephone, Cambridge blue vase of flowers, opened bottle
    of red wine, glass, bottle of pills
Waste-paper basket
Wheelchair
**Anne**'s raincoat and bag

*Off stage*:    Small package (**Gary**)
Clothing (**Julia**)
Tray of tea things (**Julia**)
Mug of coffee (**Julia**)
Small bunch of shop flowers (**Margaret**)
Blue vase with shop flowers (**Margaret**)
Cake tin (**Margaret**)
Clothing in dry cleaner's bags (**Gary**)
Glass of water (**Julia**)
Glass of water (**Margaret**)
Duster (**Gary**)

*Personal*:    **Gary**: pocket diary, key, personal stereo, duster, receipt
**Margaret**: handbag containing reading glasses, photographs
**Julia**: key

During black-out p. 7:

*Strike*:          Package from occasional table

*Re-set*:          Wheelchair

*Set*:             Gift-wrapped plant
                   **Margaret**'s bag and coat

During black-out p. 13

*Strike*:          Blue vase of flowers to kitchen

*Re-set*:          Plant

*Set*:             "Henry"-type vacuum cleaner (practical) for **Gary**
                   **Gary**'s jacket in kitchen

During black-out p. 28

*Set*:             Replace wine bottle with identical empty bottle
                   Scattering of papers by sofa
                   Chiffon scarf over sofa arm

During black-out p. 35

*Set*:             **Gary**'s jacket on newel post
                   Unsealed envelope containing banknotes on **Julia**'s desk

### ACT II

*Set*:             Bag of groceries by sofa
                   Key in door
                   Key behind books on bookshelf
                   Window curtains partially drawn

*Off stage*:       Aluminium elbow crutches, pile of mail (**Julia**)
                   Overnight bag (**Margaret**)
                   Tray with bowl of soup, slice of bread on sideplate, napkin, cutlery
                       (**Margaret**)
                   Tray of light food, glass of water (**Margaret**)
                   Rodgers and Hammerstein CD (**Margaret**)
                   Glass of water (**Margaret**)
                   Purse (**Margaret**)

*Personal*:    **Anne**: handbag
           **Margaret**: handbag containing pillbox, letters, Visa bill, other bills,
           Banham key

During black-out p. 47

*Set*:         Bottle of wine, single flower in stem vase on coffee table
           Bottle of wine
           Glass of wine for **Julia**

During black-out p. 55

*Set*:         Note

*Re-set*:      Bottle of pills on coffee table

During black-out p. 59

*Set*:         Small pillbox, medicine bottle, Kleenex tissue with several capsules on
           it on worktable

During black-out p. 65

*Set*:         Bottle of wine and part-filled glass

*Re-set*:      Cordless telephone on work table
           Chain on door

# LIGHTING PLOT

Practical fittings required: anglepoise lamp, table lamps, side lights
A sitting-room. The same throughout

ACT I

*To open*: Darkness

| | | |
|---|---|---|
| *Cue* 1 | Silence after car crash<br>*Spot on* **Julia** | (Page 2) |
| *Cue* 2 | **Julia**: " ... I can tell you." Pause<br>*Full general sunlight on room* | (Page 2) |
| *Cue* 3 | **Julia** stands looking at the envelope<br>*Black-out. When ready, bring up bright sunshine*<br>   *effect on room* | (Page 7) |
| *Cue* 4 | Mozart music swells up<br>*Black-out. When ready, bring up morning sunshine effect* | (Page 13) |
| *Cue* 5 | **Anne**: " ... you'll be to tell her." Pause<br>*Black-out. When ready bring up lighting as before* | (Page 19) |
| *Cue* 6 | **Julia** looks towards the kitchen<br>*Black-out. When ready bring up sunlight effect* | (Page 23) |
| *Cue* 7 | **Julia**: "I was fucking your husband." Pause<br>*Black-out. When ready bring up early evening light,*<br>   *anglepoise lamp on* | (Page 28) |
| *Cue* 8 | **Julia** turns on main lights<br>*Snap on main interior lights* | (Page 29) |
| *Cue* 9 | **Julia** begins working and becomes engrossed<br>*Fade interior and exterior lights to black, leaving*<br>   *anglepoise on; bring up table lamps* | (Page 32) |
| *Cue* 10 | **Julia**: "What do you want?"<br>*Black-out. When ready bring up bright sunlight effect* | (Page 32) |

| *Cue* 11 | **Margaret** goes into kitchen | (Page 35) |
| | *Black-out. When ready bring up early afternoon effect* | |

| *Cue* 12 | **Gary**: " ... all of you." Pause | (Page 37) |
| | *Black-out. When ready, bring up shadowy evening light* | |
| | *with one side light on; pause, then shaft of light* | |
| | *from upstairs window* | |

| *Cue* 13 | As **Julia** closes the door | (Page 37) |
| | *Snap off shaft of light from upstairs window* | |

| *Cue* 14 | **Julia** switches off the side light | (Page 38) |
| | *Snap off side light; pause; snap on shaft of light* | |
| | *from upstairs window; snap on narrow shaft of light* | |
| | *at top of stairs, growing wider* | |

| *Cue* 15 | The door upstairs is closed quickly | (Page 38) |
| | *Snap off shaft of light from upstairs* | |

| *Cue* 16 | Upstairs door opens | (Page 38) |
| | *Snap on narrow shaft of light from upstairs, growing wider* | |

ACT II

*To open*: Bright sunlight through window

| *Cue* 17 | Music plays | (Page 47) |
| | *Black-out. When ready, bring up evening effect* | |
| | *with practicals on* | |

| *Cue* 18 | **Margaret** exits into the kitchen | (Page 50) |
| | *Black-out. When ready, bring up morning effect* | |

| *Cue* 19 | **Julia** remains, sitting alone | (Page 52) |
| | *Black-out. When ready bring up late morning effect* | |

| *Cue* 20 | **Julia** puts her hands to her head | (Page 53) |
| | *Black-out. When ready, bring up evening effect with* | |
| | *practicals on* | |

| *Cue* 21 | **Margaret** looks down at the sleeping **Julia** | (Page 55) |
| | *Black-out. When ready bring up light in hall* | |
| | *with side light practical on* | |

| *Cue* 22 | **Julia** turns off the side light | (Page 55) |
| | *Snap off side light practical* | |

| | | |
|---|---|---|
| *Cue* 23 | **Julia** turns off the hall light<br>*Snap off to black-out. Pause, then shaft of light<br>from upstairs window* | (Page 55) |
| *Cue* 24 | Upstairs door opens<br>*Shaft of light from upstairs; pause, then black-out.<br>When ready, bring up late morning effect* | (Page 56) |
| *Cue* 25 | **Margaret**: "Please. I need help." Pause<br>*Black-out. When ready, bring up late afternoon effect* | (Page 58) |
| *Cue* 26 | **Margaret** exits to the kitchen<br>*Black-out. When ready bring up evening effect with practicals on* | (Page 62) |
| *Cue* 27 | **Julia** holding the telephone, **Margaret** by the door<br>*Fade to black-out. When ready, bring up evening effect<br>with practicals on* | (Page 65) |
| *Cue* 28 | **Margaret**: "Wonderful." A moment<br>*Black-out* | (Page 73) |
| *Cue* 29 | **Coroner's Voice**: " ... implicated in her demise —— "<br>*Spot on* **Gary**, L | (Page 73) |
| *Cue* 30 | **Gary**: " ... like I said I would —— "<br>*Spot on* **Anne**, R | (Page 74) |
| *Cue* 31 | **Anne**: " ... had deteriorated considerably since ——"<br>*Spot on* **Margaret**, C | (Page 74) |
| *Cue* 32 | **Margaret**: "She had so much to live for."<br>*Fade spots on* **Gary** *and* **Anne**. *Gradually tighten<br>spot on* **Margaret** | (Page 74) |
| *Cue* 33 | Music plays<br>*Fade slowly to Black-out* | (Page 74) |

# EFFECTS PLOT

## ACT I

| | | |
|---|---|---|
| *Cue* 13 | **Julia** resumes the search for the knife<br>*Telephone* | (Page 32) |
| *Cue* 14 | **Julia** moves towards the kitchen<br>*Telephone* | (Page 32) |
| *Cue* 15 | **Julia**: "What do you want?"<br>*Fade rain sounds and music* | (Page 32) |
| *Cue* 16 | **Julia**: "Take it — please."<br>*Doorbell* | (Page 35) |
| Cue 17 | **Gary** prepares to write<br>*Doorbell* | (Page 36) |
| *Cue* 18 | Shaft of light falls on to conservatory roof. Pause<br>*Telephone rings four times; then* **Anne***'s voice over<br>answering machine as p.37* | (Page 37) |

## ACT II

| | | |
|---|---|---|
| *Cue* 19 | **Julia**: " ... and I would never have known."<br>*Doorbell* | (Page 43) |
| *Cue* 20 | **Margaret**: "It's up to you." Pause<br>*Music: Billie Holliday, "Love for Sale" over<br>house speakers and CD player* | (Page 47) |
| *Cue* 21 | The Lights come up<br>*Fade music on house speakers so that it plays<br>from CD player alone* | (Page 47) |
| *Cue* 22 | **Margaret** switches off the music<br>*Cut music* | (Page 50) |
| *Cue* 23 | **Margaret** turns on the CD player<br>*Male vocalist sings "The Surrey With The Fringe On Top"<br>from the CD player* | (Page 61) |
| *Cue* 24 | **Margaret** turns up the volume<br>*Increase volume on CD player* | (Page 62) |
| *Cue* 25 | Black-out<br>*Fade music* | (Page 62) |

Lightning Source UK Ltd.
Milton Keynes UK
UKHW021248280520
363924UK00021B/1180